knitted pets

knitted pets

A collection of playful pets to knit from scratch

Susie Johns

First published 2012 by
Guild of Master Craftsman Publications Ltd
Castle Place, 166 High Street, Lewes,
East Sussex BN7 1XU

ISBN 978-1-86108-851-2

The publishers and author can accept no legal responsibility for any
consequences arising from the application of information, advice or
instructions given in this publication.

Disclaimer
Every effort has been made to ensure the facts presented in this
book are correct; however, the publisher would like to apologize
for any unintentional errors.

A catalogue record for this book is available from the British Library.

Publisher Jonathan Bailey
Production Manager Jim Bulley
Managing Editor Gerrie Purcell
Senior Project Editor Virginia Brehaut
Copy Editor Cath Senker
Managing Art Editor Gilda Pacitti
Design Rob Janes

Set in Frutiger
Colour origination by GMC Reprographics
Printed and bound in China by Hung Hing Offset Ltd

For my children; Josh, Lillie and Edith, who share
my love of animals, both knitted and real, and who
are a constant support and inspiration.

Where those lovable pets nestle

Introduction

Every home should have a pet – and if you don't want the responsibility of a living creature then a knitted substitute could be the next best thing. Of course, there is no reason why you shouldn't have both real pets and knitted ones too.

Knitted pets are fun to create. Whether you are a novice knitter or someone with more experience, there is a pet for you. Inexperienced knitters would be advised to begin with the Dachshund or Rabbit, which are knitted using two needles, then progress to the Mouse or the Snake, both of which, though relatively easy and quick to knit, require you to use a set of four double-pointed needles. If you are a seasoned knitter looking for a challenge, however, then you might like to tackle the Guinea pig or the Iguana first.

Most of the projects are made from double-knitting yarn, which is easy to source, and most patterns require you to knit in the round using double-pointed needles – which is not as difficult as you might think.

Because these pets are small, they are relatively quick to knit, but you will need to allow extra time for making up: stitching small pieces of knitted fabric together and stuffing them requires a degree of patience and dexterity – but it's worth it when you see the finished result. Making these pets isn't just about knitting the pieces: it is about constructing them and giving each of them a personality.

An aptitude for making novelty three-dimensional items is something that I developed through making papier-mâché models for the children's magazine *Art Attack* for 12 years, and also the demands of my own three children for cuddly toys. I had a lot of fun creating these cuddly pets and I hope you have as much enjoyment in making them.

Susie Johns

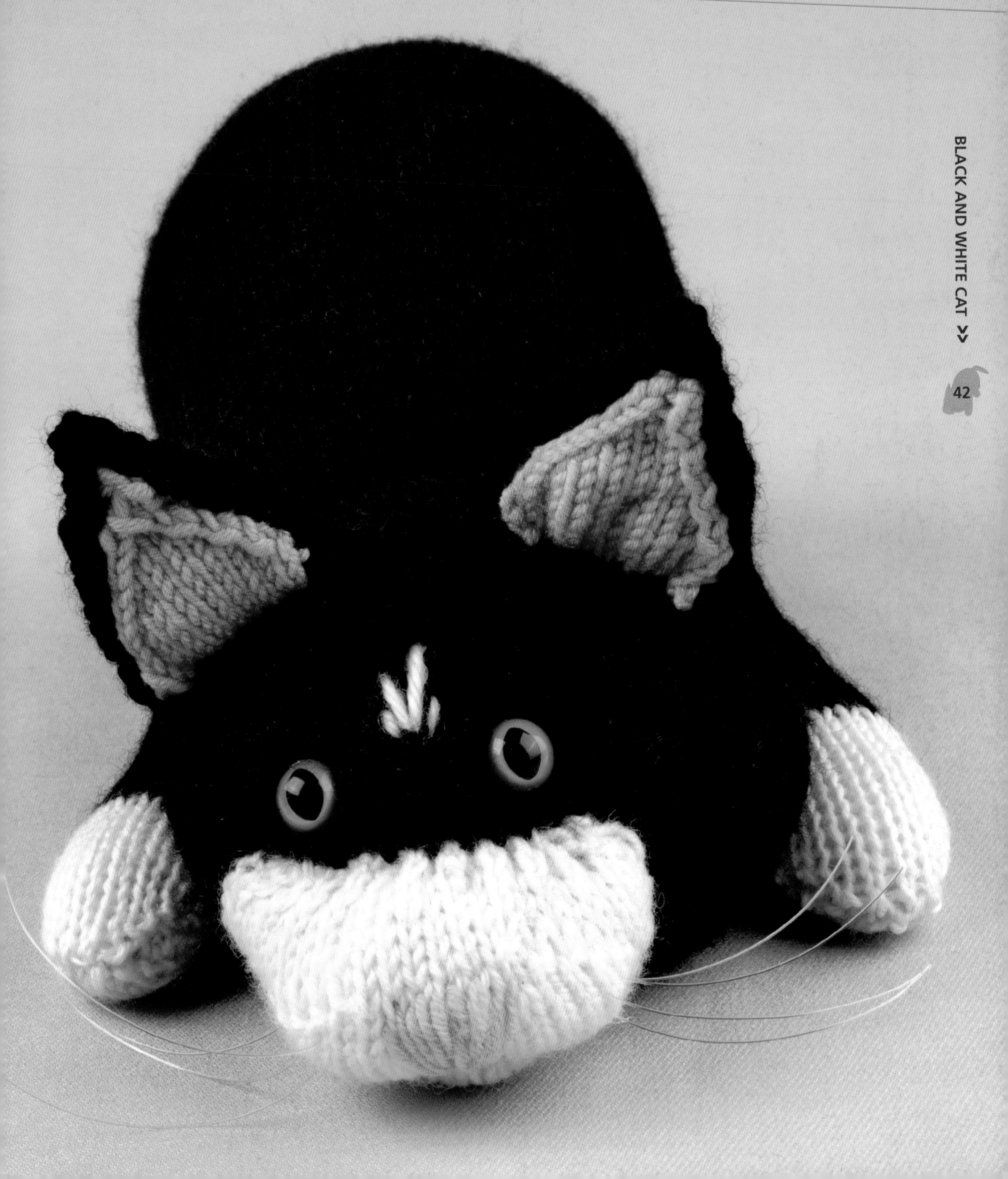

RABBIT >> 62

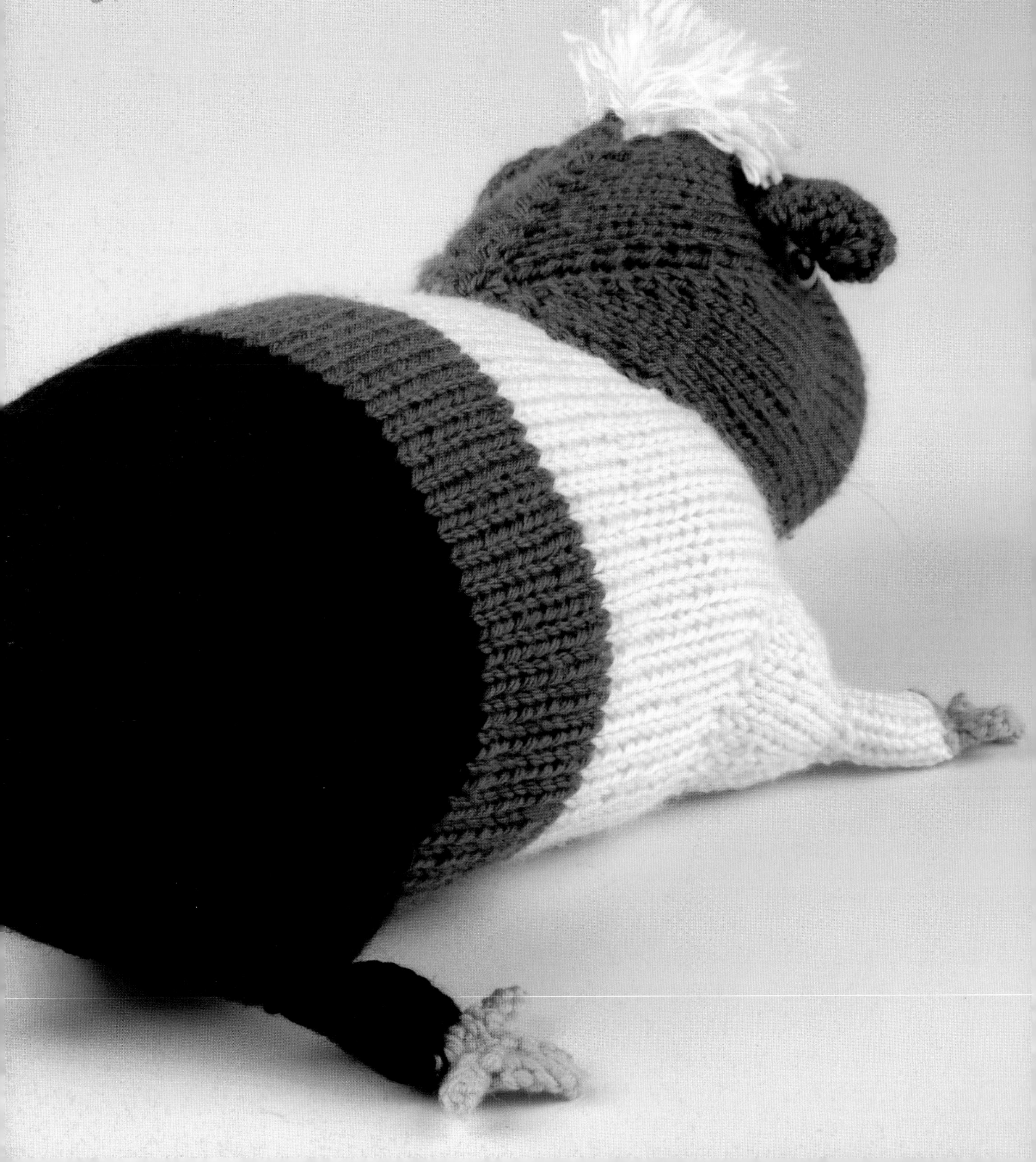

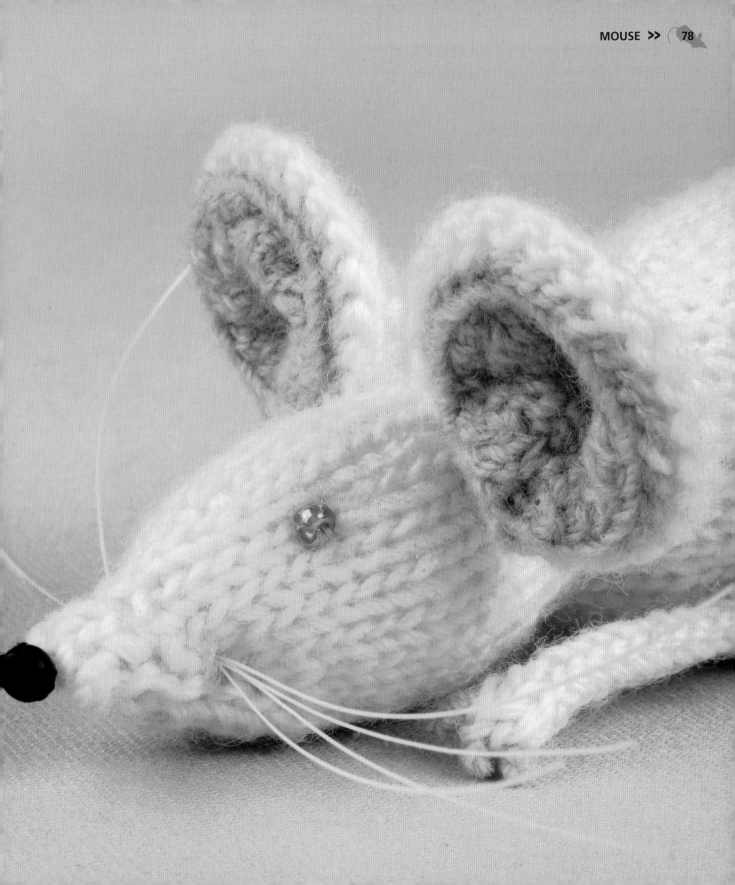

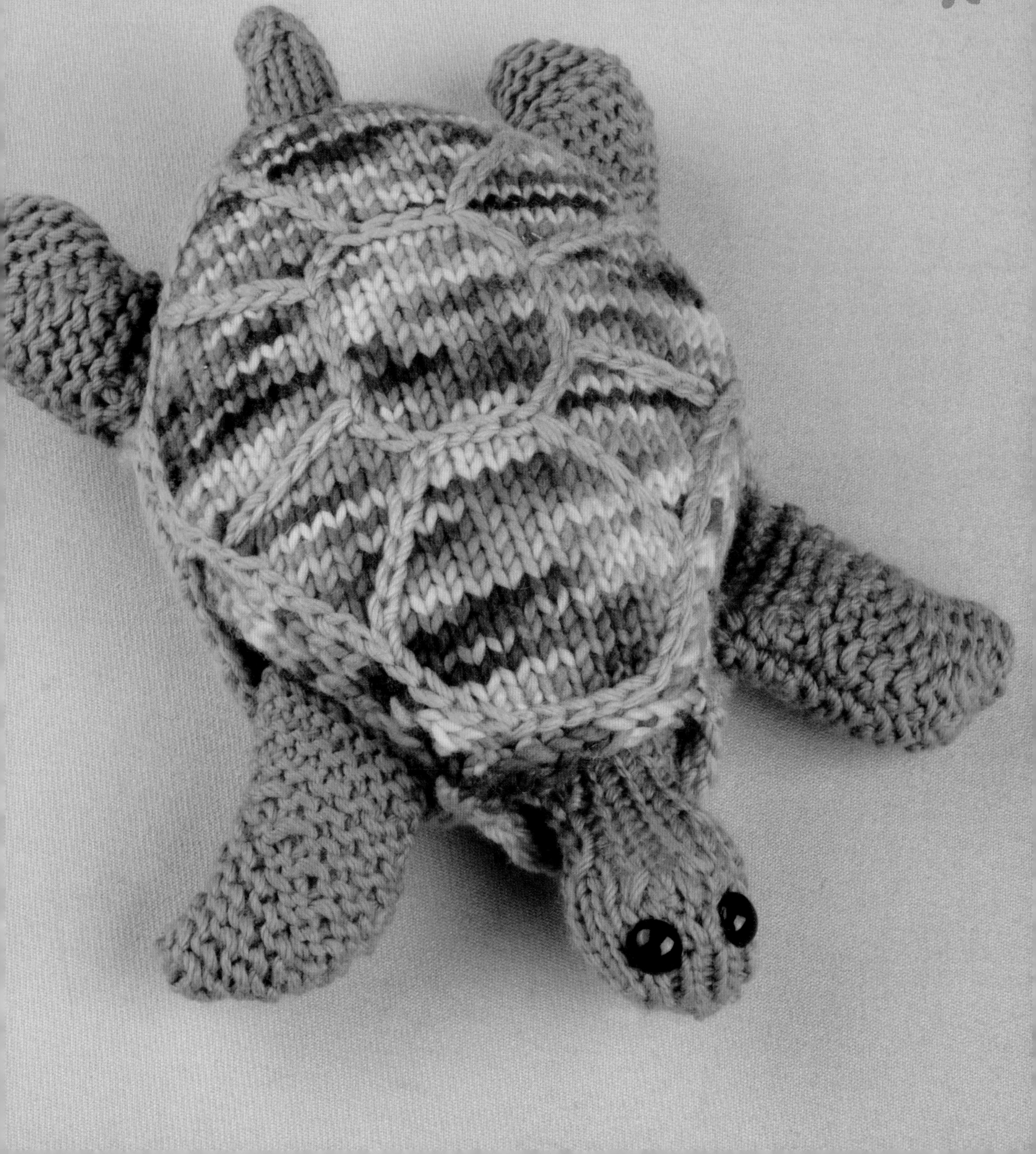

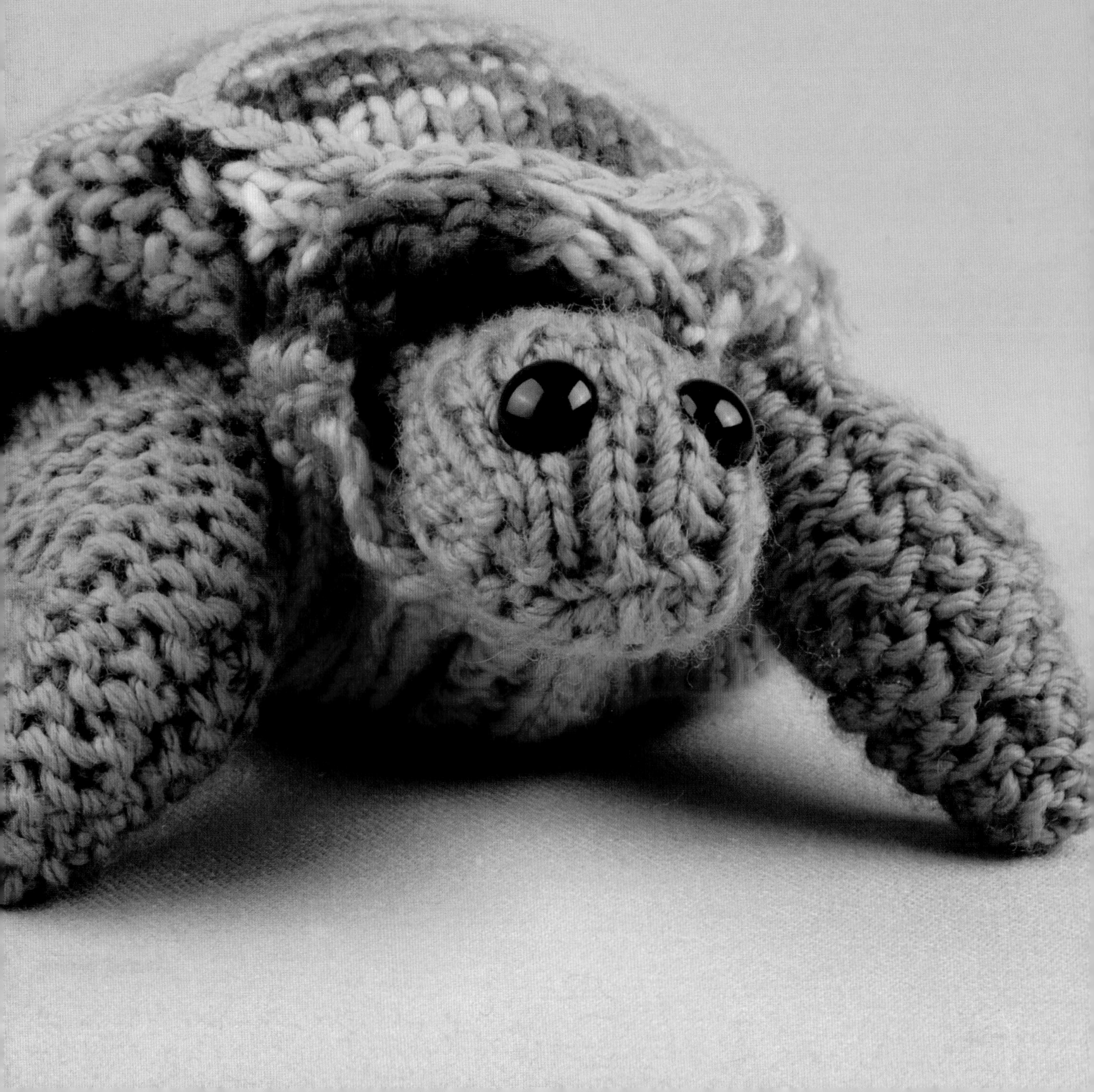

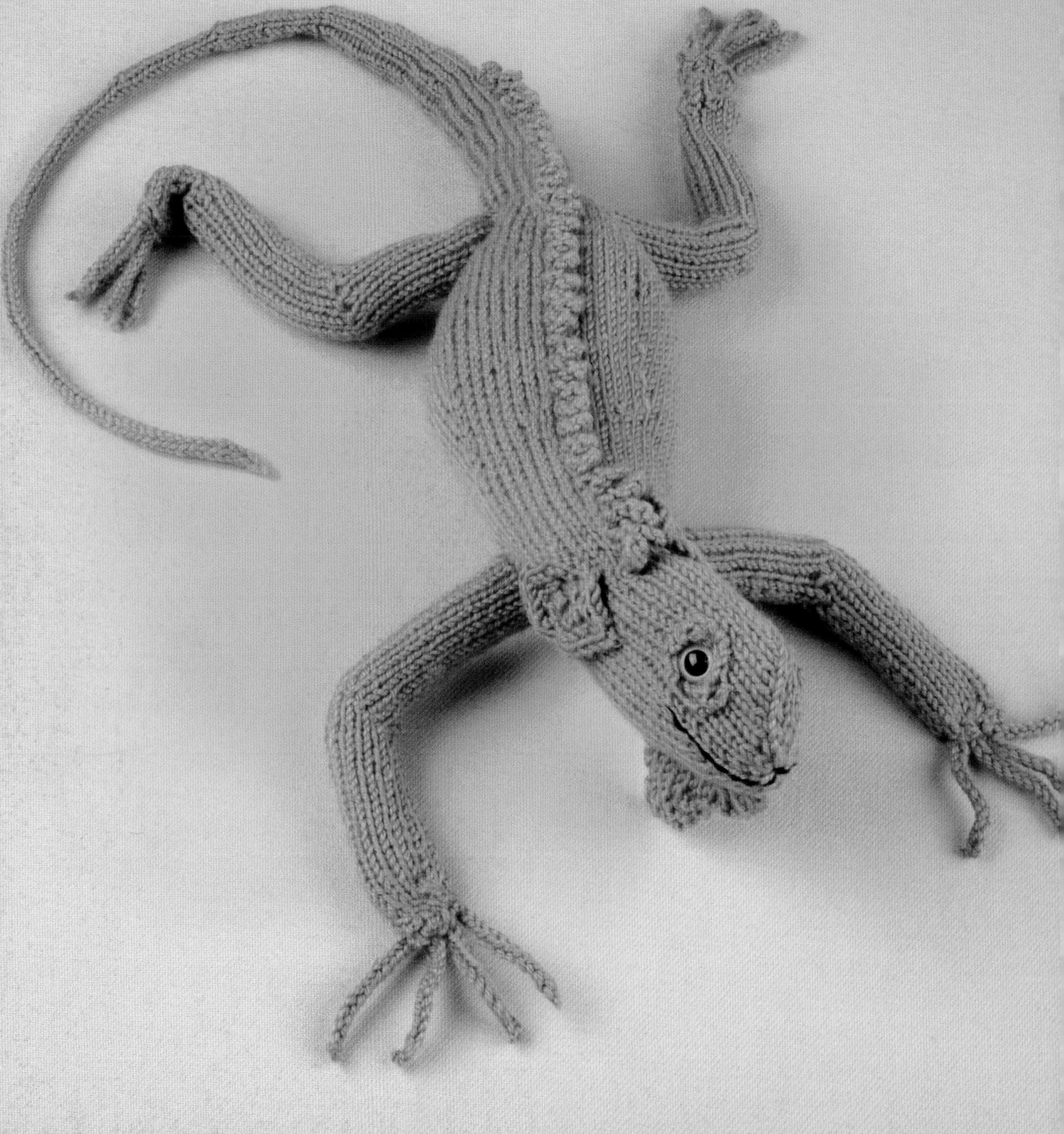

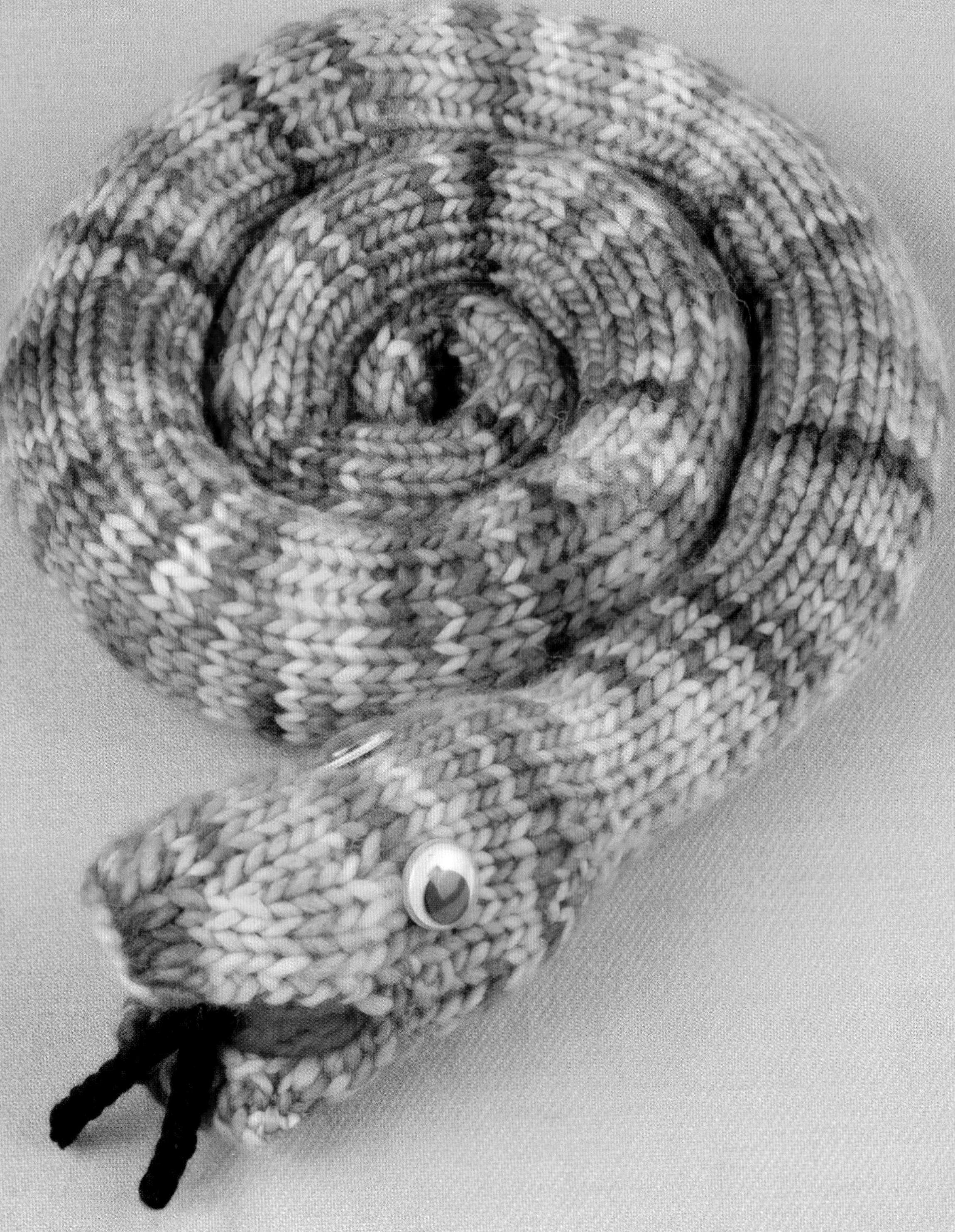

Crafty cats

Mini mice

Garish goldfish

Suspicious snakes

Lazy lizards

Pretty parrots

The Pets

Cats are popular, lovable pets that are affectionate towards their owners. Indoor cats live for an average of 15 years. They are carnivores and need plenty of meat to stay healthy. They love their naps and may sleep for up to 16 hours a day.

BLACK AND WHITE CAT

Information you'll need

Finished size

Cat measures approximately 14½in (37cm) from tip of nose to base of tail.

Materials

King Cole Merino Blend DK 100% pure new wool (123yds/112m per 50g ball)
1 x 50g ball in shade 1 White (A)
2 x 50g balls in shade 48 Black (B)
Small amount of pink DK yarn (C)
Set of four 3.25mm (UK10:US3) double-pointed needles
1 pair of 3.25mm (UK10:US3) needles
Tapestry needle
Polyester toy filling
2 x ½in (12mm) green safety eyes
Colourless nylon thread or fishing line for whiskers (optional)

Tension

24 sts and 30 rows to 4in (10cm), measured over st st, using 3.25mm needles. Use larger or smaller needles if necessary to obtain correct tension.

black and white cat

DID YOU KNOW?
Paw relations? Some people reject black and white cats – gingers are more popular.

How to make Cat

Tummy (in one piece)

Using 3.25mm needles and A, cast on
8 sts.

Row 1: Purl.

Row 2: K1, inc1, k4, inc1, k1 (10 sts).

Beg with a p row, work 5 rows in st st.

Row 8: K1, inc1, k6, inc1, k1 (12 sts).

Beg with a p row, work 17 rows in st st.

Row 26: K1, inc1, k to last 2 sts, inc1, k1
(14 sts).

Row 27: Purl.

Rep rows 26 and 27 four times more
(22 sts).

Row 36: Knit.

Row 37: Purl.

Row 38: As row 26 (24 sts).

Beg with a purl row, work 19 rows in st st.

Row 58: K1, sl1, k1, psso, k to last 3 sts,
k2tog, k1 (22 sts).

Beg with a p row, work 3 rows in st st.

Row 62: K1, sl1, k1, psso, k to last 3 sts,
k2tog, k1 (20 sts).

Row 63: Purl.

Rep rows 62 and 63 four times more
(12 sts).

Row 72: Knit.

Row 73: Purl.

Row 74: K1, sl1, k1, psso, k to last 3 sts,
k2tog, k1 (10 sts).

Beg with a purl row, work 3 rows in st st.
Cast off.

DID YOU KNOW?

There are over 500 million domestic cats in the world.

Back

Using 3.25mm needles and B, cast on
8 sts.

Row 1: Purl.

Row 2: K1, inc1, k4, inc1, k1 (10 sts).

Beg with a p row, work 5 rows in st st.

Row 8: K1, inc1, k6, inc1, k1 (12 sts).

Row 9: Purl.

Row 10: K5, (inc1) twice, k5 (14 sts).

Row 11: Purl.

Row 12: K5, inc1, k2, inc1, k5 (16 sts).

Row 13: Purl.

Row 14: K5, inc1, k4, inc1, k5 (18 sts).

Row 15: Purl.

Row 16: K5, inc1, k6, inc1, k5 (20 sts).

Row 17: Purl.

Row 18: K5, inc1, k8, inc1, k5 (22 sts).

Row 19: Purl.

Row 20: K5, inc1, k10, inc1, k5 (24 sts).

Row 21: Purl.

Row 22: K5, inc1, k12, inc1, k5 (26 sts).

Row 23: Purl.

Row 24: K5, inc1, k14, inc1, k5 (28 sts).

Row 25: Purl.

Row 26: K1, inc1, k to last 2 sts, inc1, k1
(30 sts).

Row 27: Purl.

Rep rows 26 and 27 five times more (40 sts).

Row 38: Knit.

Row 39: Purl.

Row 40: As row 26 (42 sts).

Beg with a purl row, work 19 rows in st st.

Row 60: K1, sl1, k1, psso, k to last 3 sts,
k2tog, k1 (40 sts).

Beg with a p row, work 3 rows in st st.

Row 64: K1, sl1, k1, psso, k to last 3 sts,
k2tog, k1.

Row 65: Purl.

Rep rows 64 and 65 until 12 sts rem.

Next row: K1, sl1, k1, psso, k to last 3 sts,
k2tog, k1 (10 sts).

Beg with a purl row, work 3 rows in st st.
Cast off.

Head

Using a set of four 3.25mm double-
pointed needles and B, cast on 36 sts
and divide between three needles.

Round 1: Knit.

Round 2: (K5, inc1) 6 times (42 sts).

Round 3: Knit.

Round 4: (K6, inc1) 6 times (48 sts).

Round 5: Knit.

Round 6: (K7, inc1) 6 times (54 sts).

Round 7: Knit.

Round 8: (K8, inc1) 6 times (60 sts).

Round 9: Knit.

Round 10: (K9, inc1) 6 times (66 sts).

Round 11: Knit.

Round 12: (K10, inc1) 6 times (72 sts).

Knit 10 rounds without further shaping.

Round 23: (K10, k2tog) 6 times (66 sts).

Round 24: Knit.

Round 25: (K9, k2tog) 6 times (60 sts).

Round 26: Knit.

Round 27: (K8, k2tog) 6 times (54 sts).

Round 28: Knit.

Round 29: (K7, k2tog) 6 times (48 sts).

Round 30: Knit.

Round 31: (K6, k2tog) 6 times (42 sts).

Round 32: Knit.

Round 33: (K5, k2tog) 6 times (36 sts).

Round 34: Knit.

Round 35: (K4, k2tog) 6 times (30 sts).

Round 36: Knit.

Round 37: (K3, k2tog) 6 times (24 sts).

Round 38: Knit.

Round 39: (K2, k2tog) 6 times (18 sts).

Round 40: Knit.

Round 41: (K1, k2tog) 6 times (12 sts).

Cut yarn and thread tail through rem sts.

Front paws (make one for left front paw underside and one for right front paw topside)

Using 3.25mm needles and A, cast on 6 sts.

Row 1: Purl.
Row 2: Knit.
Row 3: Purl.
Row 4: Inc1, k4, inc1 (8 sts).
Row 5: Purl.
Row 6: Inc1, k6, inc1 (10 sts).
Beg with a p row, work 7 rows in st st; cut A and join in B.
Work 16 rows in st st, using B. *
Row 30: K1, sl1, psso, k to end.
Row 31: Purl.
Rep rows 30 and 31 until 4 sts rem.
Row 42: K1, sl1, psso, k1 (3 sts).
Row 43: P1, p2tog.
Cast off rem 2 sts.

Front paws (make one for left front paw topside and one for right front paw underside)

Work as for front paws previously until *
Row 30: K to last 2 sts, k2tog, k1.
Row 31: Purl.
Rep rows 30 and 31 until 4 sts rem.
Row 42: K1, k2tog, k1 (3 sts).
Row 43: P2tog, p1.
Cast off rem 2 sts.

Back legs (make one for left back leg underside and one for right back leg topside)

Using 3.25mm needles and B, cast on 20 sts.
Beg with a p row, work 6 rows in st st.
Row 7: P2tog, p to end.
Row 8: Knit.
Rep rows 7 and 8 twice (17 sts).
Row 13: Cast off 4 sts, p to end (13 sts).
Row 14: Knit.
Row 15: As row 7 (12 sts).
Row 16: Knit.
Row 17: As row 7 (11 sts).
Row 18: Inc1, k to end.
Row 19: P2tog, p to end.
Rep rows 18 and 19 three times more.
Work 8 rows in st st.
Row 34: K1, sl1, k1, psso, k to end.
Row 35: Purl.
Rep rows 34 and 35 until 3 sts rem.
Cast off.

Back legs (make one for right back leg underside and one for left back leg topside)

Using 3.25mm needles and B, cast on 20 sts.
Beg with a p row, work 6 rows in st st.
Row 7: Purl to last 2 sts, p2tog.
Row 8: Knit.
Rep rows 7 and 8 twice (17 sts).
Row 13: Purl.
Row 14: Cast off 4 sts, k to end (13 sts).
Row 15: As row 7 (12 sts).
Row 16: Knit.
Row 17: As row 7 (11 sts).
Row 18: Knit to last st, inc1.
Row 19: Purl to last 2 sts, p2tog.
Rep rows 18 and 19 three times more.
Work 8 rows in st st.
Row 34: Knit to last 2 sts, sl1, k1, psso.
Row 35: Purl.
Rep rows 34 and 35 until 3 sts rem.
Cast off.

Paw pads (make 2)

Using 3.25mm needles and A, cast on
6 sts.
Row 1: Knit.
Row 2: Purl.
Row 3: Inc1, k4, inc1 (8 sts).
Row 4: Purl.
Row 5: Inc1, k6, inc1 (10 sts).
Beg with a p row, work 5 rows in st st.
Row 11: K2tog, k6, k2tog (8 sts).
Row 12: Purl.
Row 13: K2tog, k4, k2tog (6 sts).
Row 14: Purl.
Cast off.

Tail

Using 3.25mm needles and B, cast on
16 sts.
Beg with a p row, work 41 rows in st st;
cut B and join in A.
Work 4 rows in st st.
Row 46: (K4, k2tog) twice, k4 (14 sts).
Row 47: Purl.
Row 48: K3, k2tog, k4, k2tog, k3 (12 sts).
Row 49: Purl.
Row 50: K2, k2tog, k4, k2tog, k2 (10 sts).
Row 51: Purl.
Row 52: K1, k2tog, k4, k2tog, k1 (8 sts).
Row 53: P2tog 4 times.
Cut yarn and thread tail through rem 4 sts.

DID YOU KNOW?
The word for a cat lover
is an ailurophile.

Muzzle

Using 3.25mm needles and A, cast on
4 sts.
Row 1: Purl.
Row 2: Inc1 in each st (8 sts).
Row 3: Purl.
Row 4: K1, (inc1) twice, k2, (inc1) twice,
k1 (12 sts).
Row 5: Purl.
Row 6: K1, (inc1) twice, k6, (inc1) twice,
k1 (16 sts).
Row 7: Purl.
Row 8: K1, (inc1) twice, k10, (inc1) twice,
k1 (20 sts).
Row 9: Purl.
Row 10: K1, (inc1) twice, k14, (inc1)
twice, k1 (24 sts).
Row 11: Purl.
Row 12: K1, (inc1) twice, k18, (inc1)
twice, k1 (28 sts).

Row 13: Purl.
Row 14: K21; turn.
Row 15: P14; turn.
Row 16: K13; turn.
Row 17: P12; turn.
Row 18: K11; turn.
Row 19: P10; turn.
Row 20: K9; turn.
Row 21: P8; turn.
Row 22: K7; turn.
Row 23: P6; turn.
Row 24: K to end.
Beg with a p row, work 5 rows in st st.
Row 30: K1, sl1, k1, psso, k to last 3 sts,
k2tog, k1 (26 sts).
Row 31: Purl.
Row 32: (K2 tog) to end.
Cast off rem 13 sts purlwise.

Ears

Using 3.25mm needles and B, cast on 1 st.
Row 1: Inc2 (knit into front, back and front of st) (3 sts).
Row 2: Purl.
Row 3: K1, inc2, k1 (5 sts).
Row 4: Purl.
Row 5: (K1, inc1) twice, k1 (7 sts).
Row 6: Purl.
Row 7: K1, inc1, k3, inc1, k1 (9 sts).
Row 8: Purl.
Row 9: K1, inc1, k2, inc2, k2, inc1, k1 (13 sts).
Row 10: Purl.
Row 11: K6, inc2, k6 (15 sts).
Beg with a p row, work 7 rows in st st; cut B and join in C.

Ear lining

Row 1: K2tog, k to end (14 sts).
Row 2: P2tog, p to end (13 sts).
Beg with a k row, work 4 rows in st st.
Row 7: K1, sl1, k1, psso, k to last 3 sts, k2tog, k1.
Row 8: Purl.
Rep rows 7 and 8 three times (5 sts).
Next row: K1, sl1, k2tog, psso, k1.
Cast off rem 3 sts.

Making up

Body and legs

Join cast-on edges of tummy and back together to form back end of body. Stitch two pieces of each back leg together at side seams and stitch a paw pad to the base of each leg. Join raglan seams of legs to back end of body. Stitch two pieces of each front paw together at side seams, then join raglan seams to front of body. Stitch side seams of body, leaving front end open. Stuff body and legs firmly.

Head

Stitch muzzle to front of head and stuff head to determine finished shape before attaching eyes. Stitch head to body. On muzzle, stitch a gathering thread around lower section and pull up to shape the face, creating a chin. Fold each ear in half and stitch lining to inside of ear. Stitch ears to sides of head.

Back legs

On back legs, stitch a gathering thread around the ankle section and pull up lightly to create foot shape.

Nose

Embroider a nose using pink yarn and satin stitch. Using white yarn, embroider a few straight stitches on forehead.

Tail

Stitch tail seam; stuff tail and stitch in place.

Whiskers

For whiskers, cut lengths of fishing line or use a few bristles cut from a clean, new household brush. Dab a tiny spot of glue on one end of each whisker before inserting into knitted fabric. Trim if necessary. Omit whiskers if making this pet for a very young child.

black and white cat

47

Kittens can leave their mother and join their new family when they are between eight and twelve weeks old. A kitten needs time to adjust to its new family. It loves to play but also needs some privacy. Kittens have small stomachs and should be fed little and often.

KITTENS

DID YOU KNOW?
During her life, one female cat could have more than 100 kittens!

Information you'll need

Finished size
The kittens each measure approximately 13in (33cm) from tip of nose to end of tail and 9in (23cm) tall when standing up.

Materials
For white kitten:
King Cole Merino Blend DK 100% pure new wool (123yds/112m per 50g ball)
2 x 50g balls in shade 1 White (A)
Small amount in shade 165 Linden (F)
Small amount of pink yarn for inner ears and nose (E)

For striped kitten:
King Cole Merino Blend DK 100% pure new wool (123yds/112m per 50g ball)
1 x 50g ball in shade 1 White (A)
1 x 50g ball in shade 790 Caramel (B)
1 x 50g ball in shade 109 Copper (C)
1 x 50g ball in shade 23 Chocolate (D)
Small amount in shade 55 Gold (G)
Small amount of pink yarn for inner ears (E)
Small amount of black DK yarn

For both kittens:
1 pair of 3.25mm (UK10:US3) needles
Tapestry needle
Polyester toy filling
2 x ½in (12mm) green safety eyes
2 small bells (optional)
Colourless nylon thread or fishing line (optional)

Tension
22 sts and 30 rows to 4in (10cm), measured over st st, using 3.25mm needles. Use larger or smaller needles if necessary to obtain correct tension.

White kitten

Tummy and legs (in one piece)

Using 3.25mm needles and A, cast on
3 sts.
Beg with a p row, work 3 rows in st st.
Row 4: Inc1, k to last st, inc1 (5 sts).
Beg with a p row, work 5 rows in st st.
Row 10: Inc1, k to last st, inc1 (7 sts).
Beg with a p row, work 3 rows in st st.
Row 14: Cast on 19 sts, k to end (26 sts).
Row 15: Cast on 19 sts, p to end (45 sts).
Beg with a k row, work 8 rows in st st.
Row 24: Cast off 19 sts, k to end (26 sts).
Row 25: Cast off 19 sts, p to end (7 sts).
Beg with a k row, work 28 rows in st st.
Row 54: Cast on 19 sts, k to end (26 sts).
Row 55: Cast on 19 sts, p to end (45 sts).
Beg with a k row, work 8 rows in st st.
Row 64: Cast off 19 sts, k to end (26 sts).
Row 65: Cast off 19 sts, p to end (7 sts).

Row 66: K2tog, k to last 2 sts, k2tog
(5 sts).
Beg with a p row, work 5 rows in st st.
Row 72: K2tog, k1, k2tog (3 sts).
Row 73: Purl.
Row 74: Knit.
Row 75: P3tog; cut yarn and fasten off.

Top body and legs

Using 3.25mm needles and A, cast on
68 sts.
Beg with a k row, work 8 rows in st st.
Row 9: Cast off 19 sts, k to end (49 sts).
Row 10: Cast off 19 sts, p to end (30 sts).
Beg with a k row, work 28 rows in st st.
Row 39: Cast on 19 sts, k to end (49 sts).
Row 40: Cast on 19 sts, p to end (68 sts).
Beg with a k row, work 8 rows in st st.
Cast off.

Head

Using 3.25mm needles and A, cast on
30 sts.
Beg with a p row, work 5 rows in st st.
Row 6: (K4, inc1) 6 times (36 sts).
Row 7: (P5, inc1) 6 times (42 sts).
Row 8: (K6, inc1) 6 times (48 sts).
Row 9: (P7, inc1) 6 times (54 sts).
Beg with a k row, work 8 rows in st st.
*Shape front of head
Row 1: K47, turn.
Row 2: P40, turn.
Row 3: K39, turn.
Row 4: P38, turn.
Row 5: K37, turn.
Row 6: P36, turn.
Row 7: K35, turn.
Row 8: P34, turn.
Row 9: K33, turn.
Row 10: P32, turn.
Row 11: K31, turn
Row 12: P30, turn.
Row 13: K29, turn.
Row 14: P28, turn.
Row 15: K to end.
Row 16: Purl.
Shape top of head
Row 1: (K7, k2tog) 6 times (48 sts).
Row 2: Purl.
Row 3: (K6, k2tog) 6 times (42 sts).
Row 4: Purl.
Row 5: (K5, k2tog) 6 times (36 sts).
Row 6: Purl.
Row 7: (K4, k2tog) 6 times (30 sts).
Row 8: Purl.
Row 9: (K3, k2tog) 6 times (24 sts).
Row 10: Purl.
Row 11: (K2, k2tog) 6 times (18 sts).
Row 12: Purl.
Row 13: (K1, k2tog) 6 times (12 sts).
Row 14: (P2tog) 6 times.
Cut yarn and thread tail through rem 6 sts.

Striped kitten

Tummy

Using 3.25mm needles and A, cast on 3 sts.

Beg with a p row, work 3 rows in st st.

Row 4: Inc1, k to last st, inc1 (5 sts).

Beg with a p row, work 3 rows in st st.

Row 8: Inc1, k to last st, inc1 (7 sts).

Row 9: Purl.

Row 10: Inc1, k to last st, inc1 (9 sts).

Beg with a p row, work 53 rows in st st.

Row 64: K2tog, k to last 2 sts, k2tog (7 sts).

Beg with a p row, work 3 rows in st st.

Row 68: K2tog, k1, k2tog (5 sts).

Beg with a p row, work 3 rows in st st.

Row 72: K2tog, k1, k2tog (3 sts).

Row 73: Purl.

Row 74: Knit.

Row 75: P3tog; cut yarn and fasten off.

Top body

Using 3.25mm needles and B, cast on 30 sts.

Beg with a p row, work 3 rows in st st; do not cut B but join in C.

Beg with a k row and using C, work 3 rows in st st; do not cut C but join in D.

Beg with a p row and using D, work 3 rows in st st; do not cut D but pick up B. Continue in this way for a further 42 rows, changing colour after every 3 rows, to form a striped pattern.

Cast off.

Legs (make 4)

Using 3.25mm needles and A, cast on 18 sts.

Beg with a k row, work 6 rows in st st; cut A and join in C.

Beg with a k row and using C, work 3 rows in st st; do not cut C but join in D.

Beg with a p row and using D, work 3 rows in st st; do not cut D but join in B.

Beg with a k row and using B, work 3 rows in st st; do not cut B but pick up C.

Beg with a p row and using C, work 3 rows in st st; do not cut C but pick up D.

Beg with a k row and using D, work 3 rows in st st; cut D and pick up B.

Beg with a p row and using B, work 3 rows in st st; cut B and pick up C.

Beg with a k row and using C, work 3 rows in st st.

Cast off.

Head

Using 3.25mm needles and C, cast on 30 sts

Beg with a p row, work 3 rows in st st; do not cut C but join in B.

Beg with a k row and using B, work 3 rows in st st; do not cut B but join in D.

Beg with a p row and using D , work 3 rows in st st; do not cut D but pick up C.

Beg with a k row and using C, work 3 rows in st st; cut C and pick up B.

Beg with a p row and using B, work 3 rows in st st; cut B and pick up D.

Beg with a k row, work 2 rows in st st, then follow instructions for White kitten's head from * to end.

Both kittens

Paw pads (make 4)

Using 3.25mm needles and A, cast on 3 sts.

Row 1: Purl.

Row 2: Inc1, k1, inc1 (5 sts).

Row 3: Purl.

Row 4: Inc1, k3, inc1 (7 sts).

Row 5: Purl.

Row 6: Inc1, k5, inc1 (9 sts).

Row 7: Purl.

Row 8: K2tog, k5, k2tog (7 sts).

Row 9: Purl.

Row 10: K2tog, k3, k2tog (5 sts).

Row 11: Purl.

Row 12: K2tog, k1, k2tog (3 sts).

Cast off.

kittens

Tail

Using 3.25mm needles and A (D), cast on 12 sts.

Beg with a p row, work 41 rows in st st. For single-colour cat, continue in A; for striped cat, cut D and change to A. Work a further 4 rows in st st.

Row 46: (K2, k2tog) 3 times (9 sts).
Row 47: Purl.
Row 48: (K1, k2tog) 3 times (6 sts).
Row 49: Purl.
Row 50: (K2tog) 3 times.
Cut yarn and thread tail through rem 3 sts.

Muzzle (make 2)

Using 3.25mm needles and A, cast on 12 sts.

Row 1: Purl.
Row 2: K1, inc1, k to last 2 sts, inc1, k1 (14 sts).
Row 3: Purl.
Row 4: K12, turn.
Row 5: P10, turn.
Row 6: K9, turn.
Row 7: P8, turn.
Row 8: K7, turn.
Row 9: P6, turn.

Row 10: K5, turn.
Row 11: P4, turn.
Row 12: K to end.
Row 13: Purl.
Row 14: K1, sl1, k1, psso, k8, k2tog, k1 (12 sts).
Row 15: Purl.
Row 16: K1, sl1, k1, psso, k6, k2tog, k1 (10 sts).
Row 17: Purl.
Row 18: K1, sl1, k1, psso, k4, k2tog, k1 (8 sts).
Row 19: Purl.
Row 20: K1, sl1, k1, psso, k2, k2tog, k1 (6 sts).
Row 21: Purl.
Row 22: K1, sl1, k1, psso, k2tog, k1 (4 sts).
Row 23: P1, p2tog, p1 (2 sts).
Row 24: K2tog; cut yarn and fasten off.

Ears (make 2)

Using 3.25mm needles and A (D), cast on 12 sts.

Row 1: Purl.
Row 2: Knit.
Row 3: Purl.
Row 4: K1, sl1, k1, psso, k6, k2tog, k1 (10 sts).
Row 5: Purl.
Row 6: K1, sl1, k1, psso, k4, k2tog, k1 (8 sts).
Row 7: Purl.
Row 8: K1, sl1, k1, psso, k2, k2tog, k1 (6 sts).
Row 9: Purl.
Row 10: K1, sl1, k1, psso, k2tog, k1 (4 sts).
Row 11: P1, p2tog, p1 (2 sts).
Row 12: K2tog; cut yarn and fasten off.

Inner ears (make 2)

Using 3.25mm needles and E, cast on 10 sts.

Row 1: Knit each st tbl.
Row 2: Purl.
Row 3: K1, sl1, k1, psso, k4, k2tog, k1 (8 sts).
Row 4: Purl.
Row 5: K1, sl1, k1, psso, k2, k2tog, k1 (6 sts).
Row 6: Purl.
Row 7: K1, sl1, k1, psso, k2tog, k1 (4 sts).
Row 8: P2tog twice (2 sts).
Row 9: K2tog; cut yarn and fasten off.

Collar

Using 3.25mm needles and F (G), cast on 42 sts.

Row 1: Knit each st tbl.
Rep row 1 twice more.
Cast off, knitting each st tbl.

Making up

Body: white kitten

Join leg and body seams, leaving the bottom of each leg open. With points at each end of tummy facing upwards, join sides of points to cast-on and cast-off edges of top body. Turn right sides out and stuff firmly. Stitch a paw pad to the base of each leg.

Body: striped kitten

Join pointed ends of tummy and back together to form back end of body; leave the front end open at this stage. Stitch each leg seam and stitch a paw pad to the base of each leg. Stitch side seams of tummy and back together at centres, leaving openings to fit each of the four legs. Stitch legs in place then stuff legs and body firmly and stitch pointed end of tummy to front end (cast-off seam) of upper body.

Both kittens

To make muzzle, stitch two side edges together to form centre seam, then stitch muzzle to front of head. Stuff head to determine finished shape before attaching eyes, then stitch head to body.

Stitch each ear lining to inside of ear. Pin ears in position, then stitch ears to sides of head. Embroider a nose in satin stitch, using pink yarn for the single-colour kitten and black for the striped kitten. Using the same yarn, embroider a few straight stitches to denote mouth. Wrap collar around neck and stitch short ends together; attach bell.

Cut lengths of fishing line or use a few bristles cut from a clean, new household brush. Dab a tiny spot of glue on one end of each whisker before inserting into knitted fabric. Trim if necessary. Omit whiskers if making this pet for a very young child.

kittens

DID YOU KNOW?
It's not true that all ginger cats are male.

Dachshunds were bred to hunt alone, so they are very independent dogs. They have a strong instinct to hunt prey and will chase after any small creature – little children beware! Dachshunds are good with gentle, respectful children but should never be teased. Worth knowing: this little dog has a loud bark.

DACHSHUND

Information you'll need

Finished size

Dachshund measures approximately
15½in (40cm) from nose to tail.

Materials

Cygnet Superwash DK, 100% pure wool
(114yds/104m per 50g ball)
2 x 50g balls in shade 4315 Taupe (A)
Small amounts of DK yarn in pink (B), black
(C) and red (D)
1 pair of 3.25mm (UK10:US3) needles
Tapestry needle
Polyester toy filling
2 buttons for eyes (approx. ½in/12mm)
1 x ½in (12mm) jump ring for buckle

Tension

23 sts and 30 rows to 4in (10cm),
measured over st st using 3.25mm needles.
Use larger or smaller needles if necessary
to obtain correct tension.

DID YOU KNOW?
Dogs can hear sounds up to
four times the distance that
humans can.

DID YOU KNOW?
Slow coach: a dachshund
learns commands slowly,
so be patient with your pet.

How to make Dachshund

Left body

Using 3.25mm needles and A, cast on
48 sts.
Row 1: Knit.
Row 2: Purl.
Row 3: Knit to last st, inc1.
Rep rows 2 and 3 five times more (54 sts).
Beg with a purl row, work 5 rows in st st.
Row 19: K1, sl1, k1, psso, k to end.
Row 20: P to last 3 sts, p2tog, p1.
Rep rows 19 and 20 twice more (48 sts).
Row 25: Cast off 37 sts, k to end (11 sts).
Row 26: P to last 2 sts, p2tog.
Row 27: Knit.
Rep rows 26 and 27 once more (9 sts).
Row 30: Inc1, p to end.
Row 31: Knit.
Rep rows 30 and 31 once more (11 sts).
Row 34: Cast on 10 sts (to form nose),
p to end (21 sts).
Row 35: Knit.
Row 36: Purl.
Row 37: K to last 2 sts, k2tog (20 sts).
Row 38: P2tog, p to last 2 sts, p2tog
(18 sts).
Rep rows 37 and 38 until 3 sts remain.
Cast off purlwise.

Right body

Follow instructions for left body, reversing
shaping.

Upper body

Using 3.25mm needles and A, cast on 1 st.
Row 1: Knit.
Row 2: Inc1 purlwise (2 sts).
Row 3: Knit.
Row 4: (Inc1 purlwise) twice (4 sts).
Row 5: Knit.
Row 6: Purl.
Row 7: Inc1, k2, inc1 (6 sts).
Row 8: Purl.
Row 9: Knit.
Row 10: Inc1 purlwise, p4, inc1 purlwise
(8 sts).
Beg with a knit row, work 60 rows in st st.
Row 71: K2tog, k4, k2tog (6 sts).
Row 72: Purl.
Row 73: Knit.
Row 74: P2tog, p2, p2tog (4 sts).
Row 75: Knit.
Row 76: Purl.
Row 77: (K2tog) twice (2 sts).
Row 78: P2tog; cut yarn and fasten off.

Lower body

Follow instructions for upper body, but
after completing row 10, work 108 rows in
st st, then continue following instructions
from row 71 to end.

Front legs (make 2)

Using 3.25mm needles and A, cast on
14 sts.
Row 1: K each st tbl.
Beg with a p row, work 17 rows in st st.
Row 19: K2tog, k to last 2 sts, k2tog.
Row 20: Purl.
Rep rows 19 and 20 until 8 sts rem.
Cast off.

Back legs (make 2)

Follow instructions for front legs, but after
completing row 1, work 21 rows in st st,
then continue following instructions from
row 19 to end.

Paws (make 4)

Using 3.25mm needles and A, cast on
6 sts.
Row 1: Purl.
Row 2: Inc1, k4, inc1 (8 sts).
Beg with a p row, work 4 rows in st st.
Row 7: P2tog, p4, p2tog (6 sts).
Row 8: Knit.
Cast off.

Tail

Using 3.25mm needles and A, cast on
8 sts.
Beg with a k row, work 26 rows in st st.
Row 27: K2tog, k4, k2tog (6 sts).
Row 28: Purl.
Row 29: Knit.
Row 30: P2tog, p2, p2tog (4 sts).
Row 31: Knit.
Row 32: Purl.
Row 33: (K2tog) twice (2 sts).
Row 34: P2tog; cut yarn and fasten off.

Ears (make 2)

Using 3.25mm needles and A, cast on
10 sts.
Row 1: Knit.
Row 2: Purl.
Row 3: Inc1, k8, inc1 (12 sts).
Beg with a p row, work 15 rows in st st.
Row 19: K2tog, k to end (11 sts).
Row 20: P2tog, p to end (10 sts).
Cast off.

Ear linings (make 2)

Using 3.25mm needles and B, cast on
8 sts.

Row 1: Knit.
Row 2: Purl.
Row 3: Inc1, k6, inc1 (10 sts).
Beg with a p row, work 15 rows in st st.
Row 19: K2tog, k to end (9 sts).
Row 20: P2tog, p to end (8 sts).
Cast off.

Nose

Using 3.25mm needles and C, cast on 6 sts.
Row 1: Purl.
Row 2: Inc1, k4, inc1 (8 sts).
Beg with a p row, work 4 rows in st st.
Row 7: P2tog, p4, p2tog (6 sts).
Row 8: Knit.
Cast off, leaving a tail of yarn.

Collar

Using 3.25mm needles and D, cast on 2 sts.
Row 1: Knit.
Row 2: Purl.
Row 3: (Inc1) twice (4 sts).
Row 4: Sl1 knitwise, p2, k1.
Row 5: Sl1, k3.
Rep rows 4 and 5 until strip fits around neck with at least 1¼–1½in (3–4cm) overlap.

Making up

Body and head

Starting at the nose and with right sides facing out, stitch head seam in mattress stitch for 1½in (4cm). Pin upper body to upper edges of left and right sides from this point to the tail end, then stitch in place. Pin lower body to lower edges of sides and stitch in place, leaving a small gap in one of the seams. Stuff firmly, then stitch gap closed.

Legs

With right sides together, fold each leg in half and stitch seam in backstitch. With purl side outwards, pin and stitch paws to openings at base of each leg. Stuff legs firmly and stitch to body.

Stitch tail seam and add a little stuffing if necessary, then stitch to back end of body.

Ears

Place lining inside ear and oversew edges of ear over edges of lining all round, then stitch lined ears to sides of head.

Facial features

For nose, thread tail of yarn into tapestry needle and stitch a running stitch all around edges, then place a small piece of stuffing on wrong side and pull up yarn to gather into a ball; stitch to front of head. Sew the two buttons on either side of the head for the eyes.

Stitch buckle to ends of collar strip.

DID YOU KNOW?
Dachshunds are known as sausage dogs – or you can call them hot dogs.

Spaniels were originally bred to hunt animals. Cocker spaniels are small with a long, silky coat and ears. American water spaniels are large with curly coats. Spaniels make ideal pets: they are intelligent and love human company. They have an amazing sense of smell, so the police use them to sniff out drugs and explosives.

SPANIEL PUPPY

Information you'll need

Finished size

Puppy's body measures approximately 6in (15cm) long and, with paws outstretched, he is about 11½in (29cm) from the ends of his front paws to the tip of his tail.

Materials

Rowan Cashsoft Baby DK, 57% extra fine merino, 33% acrylic microfibre, 10% cashmere (126yds/115m per 50g ball)
2 x 50g balls in shade 800 Snowman (A)
Rowan Cashsoft DK, 57% extra fine merino, 33% acrylic microfibre, 10% cashmere (126yds/115m per 50g ball)
1 x 50g ball in shade 517 Donkey (B)
Small amount of DK yarn in red (C)
1 pair of 3.25mm (UK10:US3) needles
Tapestry needle
Polyester toy filling
2 x ½in (12mm) amber safety eyes
1 x black safety dog nose
2 x ⁹⁄₃₂in (7mm) ribbon clamps
1 x ³⁄₈in (10mm) split ring
1 x trigger clasp

Tension

22 sts and 30 rows to 4in (10cm), measured over st st, using 3.25mm needles. Use larger or smaller needles if necessary to obtain correct tension.

DID YOU KNOW?
Don't be fooled by a cocker spaniel's sad, pleading eyes. It's actually a very happy breed.

DID YOU KNOW?
It's said that King Charles II of England put up signs saying 'Beware of the Dog' – to warn people not to tread on his spaniels!

spaniel puppy

How to make Puppy

Tummy (in one piece)
Using 3.25mm needles and A, cast on 3 sts.
Beg with a p row, work 3 rows in st st.
Row 4: Inc1, k to last st, inc1 (5 sts).
Beg with a p row, work 3 rows in st st.
Row 8: Inc1, k to last st, inc1 (7 sts).
Row 9: Purl.
Row 10: Inc1, k to last st, inc1 (9 sts).
Beg with a p row, work 55 rows in st st.
Row 66: K2tog, k to last 2 sts, k2tog (7 sts).
Beg with a p row, work 3 rows in st st.
Row 70: K2tog, k to last 2 sts, k2tog (5 sts).
Beg with a p row, work 3 rows in st st.
Row 74: K2tog, k1, k2tog (3 sts).
Row 75: Purl.
Row 76: Knit.
Row 77: P3tog; cut yarn and fasten off.

Top body
Using 3.25mm needles and A, cast on 36 sts.
Beg with a p row, work 55 rows in st st.
Cast off.

Legs (make 4)
Using 3.25mm needles and A, cast on 18 sts.
Beg with a p row, work 27 rows in st st.
Row 28: K1, sl1, k1, psso, k to last 3 sts, k2tog, k1.
Row 29: Purl.
Rep rows 28 and 29 five times (6 sts).
Row 38: K1, sl1, k1, psso, k2tog, k1 (4 sts).
Cast off purlwise.

Paw pads (make 4)
Using 3.25mm needles and A, cast on 3 sts.
Row 1: Purl.
Row 2: Inc1, k1, inc1 (5 sts).
Row 3: Purl.
Row 4: Inc1, k3, inc1 (7 sts).
Row 5: Purl.
Row 6: Inc1, k5, inc1 (9 sts).
Row 7: Purl.
Row 8: K2tog, k5, k2tog (7 sts).
Row 9: Purl.
Row 10: K2tog, k3, k2tog (5 sts).
Row 11: Purl.
Row 12: K2tog, k1, k2tog (3 sts).
Cast off.

Head
Using 3.25mm needles and B, cast on 30 sts.
Beg with a p row, work 7 rows in st st.
Row 8: (K4, inc1) 6 times (36 sts).
Row 9: Purl.
Row 10: (K5, inc1) 6 times (42 sts).
Row 11: Purl.
Row 12: (K6, inc1) 6 times (48 sts).
Beg with a p row, work 3 rows in st st.
Row 16: (K6, k2tog) 6 times (42 sts).
Row 17: Purl.
Row 18: (K5, k2tog) 6 times (36 sts).
Row 19: Purl.
Row 20: (K4, k2tog) 6 times (30 sts).
Row 21: Purl.
Row 22: (K3, k2tog) 6 times (24 sts).
Row 23: (P2tog, p2) 6 times (18 sts).
Row 24: (K1, k2tog) 6 times (12 sts).
Row 25: (P2tog) 6 times.
Cut yarn and thread tail through rem 6 sts.

DID YOU KNOW?
Spaniels first came from Spain – hence the name.

Muzzle
Using 3.25mm needles and A, cast on 6 sts.
Row 1: Purl.
Row 2: K1, inc1, k2, inc1, k1 (8 sts).
Row 3: Purl.
Row 4: K1, inc1, k4, inc1, k1 (10 sts).
Row 5: Purl.
Row 6: Knit.
Row 7: Cast on 6 sts, p to end (16 sts).
Row 8: Cast on 6 sts, k to end (22 sts).
Row 9: Purl.
Row 10: K1, inc1, k to last 2 sts, inc1, k1 (24 sts).
Beg with a p row, work 11 rows in st st.
Row 22: Cast off 10 sts, k to end (14 sts).
Row 23: Cast off 10 sts, p to end (4 sts).
Beg with a k row, work 36 rows in st st.
Cast off.

Ears (make 2)
Using 3.25mm needles and B, cast on 9 sts.
Row 1: Knit each st tbl.
Row 2: K2, p5, k2.
Row 3: K1, inc1, k to last 2 sts, inc1, k2.
Row 4: K2, p to last 2 sts, k2.
Rep rows 3 and 4 twice more (15 sts).
Row 9: K1, inc1, k5, inc2 in next stitch, k5 inc1, k1 (19 sts).
Row 10: K2, p to last 2 sts, k2.
Row 11: Knit.
Rep rows 10 and 11 three times and row 10 once more.
Row 19: K1, (sl1, k1, psso, k3) twice, k2tog, k3, k2tog, k1 (15 sts).
Row 20: K2, p to last 2 sts, k2.
Row 21: Knit.
Row 22: K2, p to last 2 sts, k2.
Row 23: K1, sl1, k1, psso, k3, sl1, k2tog, psso, k3, k2tog, k1 (11 sts).
Row 24: K2, p to last 2 sts, k2.
Row 25: Knit.

Row 26: K2, p to last 2 sts, k2.
Row 27: K1, sl1, k1, psso, k5, k2tog, k1
(9 sts).
Row 28: K2, p to last 2 sts, k2.
Row 29: K1, sl1, k1, psso, k3, k2tog, k1
(7 sts).
Rows 30–32: as rows 24–26.
Cast off.

Tail

Using 3.25mm needles and A, cast on 16 sts.
Beg with a p row, work 3 rows in st st.
Row 4: K1, sl1, k1, psso, k4, (inc1) twice, k4,
k2tog, k1.
Row 5: Purl.
Rep rows 4 and 5 once.
Row 8: K1, sl1, k1, psso, k10, k2tog, k1
(14 sts).
Row 9: Purl.
Row 10: K1, sl1, k1, psso, k3, (inc1) twice,
k3, k2tog, k1.
Row 11: Purl.
Rep rows 10 and 11 twice.
Row 16: K1, sl1, k1, psso, k8, k2tog, k1
(12 sts).
Row 17: Purl.
Row 18: K1, sl1, k1, psso, k2, (inc1) twice,
k2, k2tog, k1.
Row 19: Purl.
Row 20: K1, sl1, k1, psso, k6, k2tog, k1
(10 sts).
Row 21: Purl.
Row 22: K1, sl1, k1, psso, k4, k2tog, k1
(8 sts).
Row 23: Purl.
Row 22: K1, sl1, k1, psso, k2, k2tog, k1.
Cut yarn and thread tail through rem 6 sts.

Collar

Using 3.25mm needles and C, cast on 42 sts.
Row 1: Knit each st tbl.
Rep row 1 twice more.
Cast off, knitting each st tbl.

Lead

Using 3.25mm needles and C, cast on
200 sts.
Row 1: Knit each st tbl.
Cast off, knitting each st tbl.

Making up

Body

Join pointed ends of tummy and back
together to form back and front ends of
body. Stitch each leg seam and stitch a paw
pad to the base of each leg. Pin side seams
of tummy and back together at centres.
Stitch front legs in place, matching leg seams
to base of gusset seam and joining raglan
tops of each leg to opening in body. Stitch
back legs in place, with point of raglan at top
of leg a few rows along from where cast-on
edge of back joins tummy gusset. Take out
pins from centre points and turn right sides
out, then stuff legs and body firmly and
stitch openings closed.

Muzzle

To make muzzle, stitch two side edges
together to form centre seam under chin,
then stitch front flap to cast-on edges on
each side. Stuff muzzle to determine finished
shape and position nose, then remove
stuffing temporarily and fix nose in place.
Replace stuffing then stitch muzzle to front
of head, leaving the long head strip
unstitched at this stage.

Head

Stuff head before positioning eyes, then
attach eyes; stuff head firmly and stitch
head to body. Pin and stitch head strip along
centre of head, stretching slightly to fit. Press
ears using a damp cloth, then pin ears in
position before stitching to sides of head.

Tail

Stitch seam on tail, stuff and stitch in place.

Embroidery

Apply puppy's markings using Swiss darning
technique, losing any tails of yarn in the
stuffing of the body.

Attach ribbon clamps to each end of collar,
place it round puppy's neck and link the two
clamps with a split ring. Stitch the trigger
clasp to one end of the lead. Fold over the
other end to form a loop large enough to fit
around your hand, and stitch end in place.

spaniel puppy

Q: What do you get if you
cross a dog with a trampoline?
A: A springer spaniel.

These wonderful pets have soft, velvety fur and enjoy it when you gently stroke them. A rabbit's teeth will never stop growing and they love to chew on anything they can find. Rabbits are very clean animals and will groom themselves regularly.

RABBIT

Information you'll need

Finished size
Rabbit's height when seated (excluding ears) is 9½in (24cm).

Materials
Debbie Bliss Andes (DK) 65% baby alpaca, 35% mulberry silk (109yds/100m per 50g ball)
3 x 50g balls in shade 005 Fawn (A)
1 x 50g ball of merino wool yarn in dusty pink (B)
Small amounts of DK yarn in white (C) and pale green (E)
1 x 50g ball of smooth cotton yarn in orange (D)
Small amount of 4-ply yarn in black
1 pair of 3mm (UK11:US2–3) needles
Tapestry needle
Polyester toy filling
Wire brush or teasel

Tension
26 sts and 30 rows to 4in (10cm) measured over st st, using 3mm needles. Use larger or smaller needles if necessary to obtain correct tension.

rabbit

How to make Rabbit

Body (make 2)

Using 3mm needles and A, cast on 16 sts.

Row 1: Knit.

Row 2 (and each WS row): Purl.

Row 3: K1, inc1, k12, inc1, k1 (18 sts).

Row 5: K2, inc1, k12, inc1, k2 (20 sts).

Row 7: K3, inc1, k12, inc1, k3 (22 sts).

Row 9: K4, inc1, k12, inc1, k4 (24 sts).

Row 11: K5, inc1, k12, inc1, k5 (26 sts).

Row 13: K6, inc1, k12, inc1, k6 (28 sts).

Row 15: K7, inc1, k12, inc1, k7 (30 sts).

Beg with a purl row, work 25 rows in st st.

Row 41: K1, sl1, k1, psso, k24, k2tog, k1 (28 sts).

Row 43: K1, sl1, k1, psso, k22, k2tog, k1 (26 sts).

Row 45: K1, sl1, k1, psso, k20, k2tog, k1 (24 sts).

Row 47: K1, sl1, k1, psso, k18, k2tog, k1 (22 sts).

Row 49: K1, sl1, k1, psso, k16, k2tog, k1 (20 sts).

Row 51: K1, sl1, k1, psso, k14, k2tog, k1 (18 sts).

Row 53: K1, sl1, k1, psso, k12, k2tog, k1 (16 sts).

Row 55: K1, sl1, k1, psso, k10, k2tog, k1 (14 sts).

Row 57: Purl.

Cast off.

Head

Using 3mm needles and A, cast on 8 sts.

Row 1: Inc1 in each st (16 sts).

Row 2 (and each WS row): Purl.

Row 3: (K1, inc1) 8 times (24 sts).

Row 5: (K2, inc1) 8 times (32 sts).

Row 7: (K3, inc1) 8 times (40 sts).

Row 9: (K4, inc1) 8 times (48 sts).

Beg with a p row, work 21 rows in st st.

Row 31: (K4, k2tog) 8 times (40 sts).

Row 33: (K3, k2tog) 8 times (32 sts).

Row 35: (K2, k2tog) 8 times (24 sts).

Row 37: (K1, k2tog) 8 times (16 sts).

Row 39: (K2tog) 8 times.

Cut yarn and thread through rem 8 sts.

Front paws (make 2)

Using 3mm needles and A, cast on 5 sts.

Row 1: Inc1 in each st (10 sts).

Row 2: Purl.

Row 3: Inc1 in each st (20 sts).

Beg with a p row, work 15 rows in st st.

Row 19: K15; turn.

Row 20: P10; turn.

Row 21: K9; turn.

Row 22: P8; turn.

Row 23: K7; turn.

Row 24: P6; turn.

Row 25: Knit to end.

Beg with a p row, work 9 rows in st st.

Row 35: (K2tog) 10 times (10 sts).

Row 36: Purl.

Row 37: (K2tog) 5 times.

Cut yarn and thread through rem 5 sts.

Back legs (make 2)

Using 3mm needles and A, cast on 5 sts.
Row 1: Inc1 in each st (10 sts).
Row 2: Purl.
Row 3: Inc1 in each st (20 sts).
Beg with a p row, work 15 rows in st st.
Row 19: K17; turn.
Row 20: P14; turn.
Row 21: K13; turn.
Row 22: P12; turn.
Row 23: K11; turn.
Row 24: P10; turn.
Row 25: K9; turn.
Row 26: P8; turn.
Row 27: K7; turn.
Row 28: P6; turn.
Row 29: Knit to end.
Beg with a p row, work 3 rows in st st.
Row 33: K2, (inc1, k3) 4 times, inc1, k1
(25 sts).
Beg with a p row, work 3 rows in st st.
Row 37: K2, (inc1, k4) 4 times, inc1, k2
(30 sts).
Beg with a p row, work 3 rows in st st.
Row 41: K1, inc1, k to last 2 sts, inc1, k1.
Row 42: Purl.
Rep rows 41 and 42 twice more (36 sts).
Beg with a k row, work 4 rows in st st.
Row 51: K2, (k2tog, k4) 5 times, k2tog,
k2 (30 sts).
Row 52: Purl
Row 53: K2, (k2tog, k3) 5 times, k2tog,
k1 (24 sts).
Row 54: Purl.

Row 55: (K2, k2tog) 6 times (18 sts).
Row 56: Purl.
Row 57: (K1, k2tog) 6 times (12 sts).
Row 58: Purl.
Row 59: (K2tog) 6 times.
Cut yarn and thread through rem 6 sts.

Ears (make 2)

Using 3mm needles and A, cast on 5 sts.
Row 1: Knit each st tbl.
Row 2: Purl.
Row 3: Inc1 in each st (10 sts).
Beg with a p row, work 3 rows in st st.
Row 7: K1, inc1, k6, inc1, k1 (12 sts).
Beg with a p row, work 3 rows in st st.
Row 11: K1, inc1, k8, inc1, k1 (14 sts).
Beg with a p row, work 13 rows in st st.

Row 25: K1, sl1, k1, psso, k8, k2tog, k1
(12 sts).
Row 26: Purl.
Row 27: K1, sl1, k1, psso, k6, k2tog, k1
(10 sts).
Row 28: Purl.
Row 29: K1, sl1, k1, psso, k4, k2tog, k1
(8 sts).
Row 30: Purl.
Row 31: K1, sl1, k1, psso, k2, k2tog, k1
(6 sts).
Row 32: Purl.
Row 33: K1, sl1, k1, psso, k2tog, k1
(4 sts).
Row 34: Purl.
Row 35: (K2tog) twice.
Row 36: Purl.
Cast off.

BOING! If you knit a rabbit, you'll get a woolly jumper!

DID YOU KNOW?
Rabbits are very fast runners and the highest recorded jump is 3ft (90cm) high.

Ear linings (make 2)
Using 3mm needles and B, cast on 5 sts.
Row 1: Knit each st tbl.
Row 2: Purl.
Row 3: Inc1 in each st (10 sts).
Beg with a p row, work 3 rows in st st.
Row 7: K1, inc1, k6, inc1, k1 (12 sts).
Beg with a p row, work 15 rows in st st.
Row 23: K1, sl1, k1, psso, k6, k2tog, k1 (10 sts).
Beg with a p row, work 3 rows in st st.
Row 27: K1, sl1, k1, psso, k4, k2tog, k1 (8 sts).
Row 28: Purl.
Row 29: K1, sl1, k1, psso, k2, k2tog, k1 (6 sts).
Row 30: Purl.
Row 31: K1, sl1, k1, psso, k2tog, k1 (4 sts).
Row 32: Purl.
Row 33: (K2tog) twice.
Cast off purlwise.

Tail
Using 3mm needles and A, cast on 5 sts.
Row 1: Knit each st tbl.
Row 2: Purl.
Row 3: Inc1 in each st (10 sts).
Beg with a p row, work 5 rows in st st.
Row 9: K1, inc1, k6, inc1, k1 (12 sts).
Beg with a p row, work 5 rows in st st.
Row 15: K1, sl1, k1, psso, k6, k2tog, k1 (10 sts).
Row 16: P1, p2tog, p4, p2tog, p1 (8 sts).
Row 17: K1, sl1, k1, psso, k2, k2tog, k1 (6 sts).
Row 18: P1, (p2tog) twice, p1 (4 sts).
Row 19: (K2tog) twice.
Row 20: P2tog.
Cut yarn and fasten off.
Make another in the same way but using yarn C.

Carrot

Using 3mm needles and D, cast on 1 st.
Row 1: Inc2 (knit into front, back and front of st) (3 sts).
Beg with a p row, work 5 rows in st st.
Row 7: Inc1 in each st (6 sts).
Beg with a p row, work 5 rows in st st.
Row 13: Inc1 in each st (12 sts).
Beg with a p row, work 5 rows in st st.
Row 19: (K1, inc1) 6 times (18 sts).
Beg with a p row, work 5 rows in st st.
Row 25: (K2, inc1) 6 times (24 sts).
Beg with a p row, work 17 rows in st st.
Row 43: (K2, k2tog) 6 times (18 sts).
Row 44: Purl.
Row 45: (K1, k2tog) 6 times (12 sts).
Row 46: (P2tog) 6 times (6 sts).
Row 47: (K2tog) 3 times (3 sts); cut yarn and join in E.
Beg with a p row, work 11 rows in st st.
Cast off.

Making up
Body and head

To make up the body, join the two pieces at the sides. Run a length of yarn through each stitch of cast-on edges and pull up tightly to close gap; leave the opposite (neck) end open. For head, stitch seam beginning at last row and leave a 2½in (6cm) gap in the seam at the neck end. Stuff the body and head quite firmly, then stitch the head opening to the neck opening, stitch by stitch.

Legs and tail

Stitch seams on front paws and back legs and stuff before closing seams, then stitch to body, over side seams. Stitch two tail pieces together, leaving cast-on edges open, then stuff and oversew opening. Stitch to back of body, lining up the base of the tail with the gathered cast-on edge and having the white side of the tail facing outwards. Brush the white fabric with a wire brush or teasel to make it fluffy.

rabbit

Ears

Place one ear lining inside each ear, with wrong sides together, then fold edges of ears over edges of lining and oversew neatly. Gather the base of each ear slightly and stitch this edge to the top of the head.

Facial features

Using black 4-ply yarn, embroider eyes and nose in satin stitch and mouth in backstitch.

Carrot

Stitch seam on carrot, adding stuffing before closing seam. Fold stem over and sew cast-off stitches to base of stem; oversew edges tightly.

Guinea pigs are friendly creatures that enjoy being handled and love to play. They are quite nervous animals, so treat them gently. Guinea pigs are happy living in a large, wooden hutch with an outdoor run where they can exercise. They communicate using a variety of sounds, each of which has a different meaning.

GUINEA PIG

Information you'll need

Finished size

Guinea pig measures approximately
10½in (27cm) long.

Materials

Rowan Cashsoft DK yarn, 57% extra fine
merino, 33% acrylic microfibre, 10%
cashmere (126yds/115m per 50g ball)
1 x 50g ball in shade 00519 Black (A)
1 x 50g ball in shade 00517 Donkey (B)
1 x 50g ball in shade 00800 Ivory (C)
Small amount of pink DK yarn (D)
Set of four 3.25mm (UK10:US3)
double-pointed needles
1 pair of 3.25mm (UK10:US3) needles
Tapestry needle
Polyester toy filling
2 x ⅜in (10mm) blue safety eyes
Colourless nylon thread or
fishing line

Tension

24 sts and 30 rows to 4in (10cm),
measured over st st, using 3.25mm
needles. Use larger or smaller needles
if necessary to obtain correct tension.

DID YOU KNOW?
Dressed for dinner: at the Festival of the
Guinea Pig in Huacho, Peru, guinea pigs
are dressed up as kings and peasants.

How to make Guinea pig

Body (in one piece)

Using two 3.25mm double-pointed needles and A, cast on 1 st.

Row 1: Inc2 (3 sts).
Row 2: Purl.
Row 3: Knit.
Row 4: Purl.
Row 5: Inc1 in each st (6 sts).
Row 6: Purl.

Distribute sts between three needles, using fourth needle to knit, and proceed working in rounds.

Round 1: (Inc1, k1) 3 times (9 sts).
Rounds 2, 3 and 4: Knit.

Round 5: Inc1 in each st (18 sts).
Round 6: (K2, inc1) 6 times (24 sts).
Round 7: (K3, inc1) 6 times (30 sts).
Round 8: (K4, inc1) 6 times (36 sts).
Round 9: Knit.
Round 10: (Inc1, k5) twice, (k5, inc1) twice, k12 (40 sts).
Round 11: (Inc1, k6) twice, (k6, inc1) twice, k12 (44 sts).
Round 12: (Inc1, k7) twice, (k7, inc1) twice, k12 (48 sts).
Round 13: (Inc1, k5) 3 times, (k5, inc1) 3 times, k12 (54 sts).
Round 14: Knit.
Round 15: (Inc1, k6) 3 times, (k6, inc1) 3 times, k12 (60 sts).
Round 16: Knit.
Round 17: (Inc1, k7) 3 times, (k7, inc1) 3 times, k12 (66 sts).

Begin working in short rows, as follows:

Row 1: K53, turn.
Row 2: P52, turn.

Row 3: K51, turn.
Row 4: P50, turn.
Row 5: K49, turn.
Row 6: P48, turn.
Row 7: K47, turn.
Row 8: P46, turn.
Row 9: K45, turn.
Row 10: P44, turn.
Row 11: K43, turn.
Row 12: P42, turn.
Row 13: K41, turn.
Row 14: P40, turn.
Row 15: K39, turn.
Row 16: P38, turn.
Row 17: K37, turn.
Row 18: P36, turn.
Row 19: K57; do not turn but resume working in rounds.
Round 1: Knit; cut A and join in B. Knit 20 rounds.
Round 22: (K9, k2tog) 6 times (60 sts).
Round 23: Knit.

Round 24: (K8, k2tog) 6 times (54 sts).
Round 25: Knit.
Round 26: (K7, k2tog) 6 times (48 sts).
Round 27: Knit.
Round 28: (K6, k2tog) 6 times (42 sts).
Round 29: Knit.
Round 30: (K5, k2tog) 6 times (36 sts).
Round 31: Knit.
Round 32: (K4, k2tog) 6 times (30 sts).
Round 33: Knit.
Round 34: (K3, k2tog) 6 times (24 sts).
Round 35: Knit.
Round 36: (K2, k2tog) 6 times (18 sts).
Round 37: Knit.
Round 38: (K1, k2tog) 6 times (12 sts).
Round 39: Knit.
Round 40: (K2tog) 6 times.
Cut yarn, leaving a tail, and thread through rem 6 sts.

Head
Using 3.25mm needles and C, cast on 12 sts.
Row 1: Purl.
Row 2: Knit.
Row 3: Purl.
Row 4: K1, sl1, psso, k6, k2tog, k1 (10 sts).
Row 5: Purl.
Row 6: K1, sl1, psso, k4, k2tog, k1 (8 sts).
Row 7: Purl.
Row 8: K1, sl1, psso, k2, k2tog, k1 (6 sts).
Row 9: Purl.
Row 10: With RS facing, join yarn B to 1st st of cast-on row then pick up and knit 8 sts up side of work; with C, knit 6; with B (use separate ball of yarn), pick up and knit 8 sts down other side, ending at end of cast-on row (22 sts).
Row 11: P8 in B; p6 in C; p8 in B.

Row 12: Using B, k1, inc1, k6; using C k6; using B k6, inc1, k1 (24 sts).
Row 13: P9 in B; p6 in C; p9 in B.
Row 14: Using B, k1, inc1, k7; using C k6; using B k7, inc1, k1 (26 sts).
Row 15: P10 in B; p6 in C; p10 in B.
Row 16: Using B, k1, inc1, k8; using C k6; using B k8, inc1, k1 (28 sts).
Row 17: P11 in B; p6 in C; p11 in B.
Row 18: Using B, k1, inc1, k9; using C k6; using B k9, inc1, k1 (30 sts).
Row 19: P12 in B; p6 in C; p12 in B.
Row 20: Using B, k1, inc1, k10; using C k6; using B k10, inc1, k1 (32 sts).
Row 21: P13 in B; p6 in C; p13 in B.
Row 22: Using B, k1, inc1, k11; using C k6; using B k11, inc1, k1 (34 sts).
Row 23: P14 in B; p6 in C; p14 in B.

Row 24: Using B, k1, inc1, k12; using C k6; using B k12, inc1, k1 (36 sts).

Row 25: P15 in B; p6 in C; p15 in B.

Row 26: Using B, k1, inc1, k13; using C k6; using B k13, inc1, k1 (38 sts).

Row 27: P16 in B; p6 in C; p16 in B.

Row 28: Using B, k1, inc1, k14; using C k6; using B k14, inc1, k1 (40 sts).

Row 29: P17 in B; p6 in C; p17 in B.

Row 30: Using B, k1, inc1, k15; using C k6; using B k15, inc1, k1 (42 sts).

Row 31: P18 in B; p6 in C; p18 in B.

Row 32: Using B, k1, inc1, k16; using C k6; using B k16, inc1, k1 (44 sts).

Row 33: P19 in B; p6 in C; p19 in B.

Row 34: Using B, k1, inc1, k17; using C k6; using B k17, inc1, k1 (46 sts).

Row 35: P20 in B; p6 in C; p20 in B.

Row 36: Using B, k1, inc1, 18; using C k6; using B k18, inc1, k1 (48 sts).

Row 37: P21 in B, p6 in C, p21 in B.

Row 38: Using B, k1, inc1, k19; using C k6; using B k19, inc1, k1 (50 sts).

Row 39: P22 in B; p6 in C; p22 in B.

Row 40: Using B k1, sl1, k1, psso, k18, inc1; using C k6; using B inc1, k18, k2tog, k1.

Repeat rows 39 and 40 5 times more.

Row 51: P22 in B; using C p2tog, p2, p2tog tbl; p22 in B (48 sts).

Row 52: Using B (k9, sl1, k1, psso) twice; using C k4; using B (k2tog, k9) twice (44 sts).

Row 53: P20 in B; p4 in C; p20 in B.

Row 54: Using B (k8, sl1, k1, psso) twice; using C sl1, k1, psso, k2tog; using B (k2tog, k8) twice (38 sts).

Row 55: P18 in B; p2 in C; p18 in B.

Row 56: Using B (k7, sl1, k1, psso) twice; using C k2; using B (k2tog, k7) twice (34 sts); cut yarn C.

Row 57: Using B p15, p2tog, p2tog tbl, p to end (32 sts).

Row 58: (K6, sl1, k1, psso) twice, (k2tog, k6) twice (28 sts).

Row 59: Purl.

Row 60: (K5, sl1, k1, psso) twice, (k2tog, k5) twice (24 sts).

Row 61: Purl.

Row 62: (K4, sl1, k1, psso) twice, (k2tog, k4) twice (20 sts).

Row 63: Purl.

Row 64: (K3, sl1, k1, psso) twice, (k2tog, k3) twice (16 sts).

Row 65: Purl.

Row 66: (K2, sl1, k1, psso) twice, (k2tog, k2) twice (12 sts).

Row 67: Purl.

Row 68: (K1, sl1, k1, psso) twice, (k2tog, k1) twice (8 sts).

Row 69: Purl.

Row 70: (Sl1, k1, psso) twice, (k2tog) twice. Cut yarn and thread tail through rem 4 sts.

Ears (make 2)

Using 3.25mm needles and B, cast on 3 sts.

Row 1: Knit.

Row 2: K1, inc1, k1 (4 sts).

Row 3: Knit.

Row 4: K1, (inc1) twice, k1 (6 sts).

Row 5: Knit.

Row 6: K2, (inc1) twice, k2 (8 sts).

Row 7: Knit.

Row 8: K3, (inc1) twice, k3 (10 sts).

Knit 4 rows.

Row 13: K8, turn.

Row 14: K6, turn.

Row 15: K5, turn.

Row 16: K4, turn.

Row 17: K3, turn.

Row 18: K2, turn.

Row 19: K1, turn and knit to end.

Row 20: K1, sl1, k1, psso, k4, k2tog, k1 (8 sts).

Row 21: (K2tog) 4 times.

Cast off.

Legs (make 2 in A and 2 in C)

Using 3.25mm needles, cast on 8 sts. Beg with a k row, work 9 rows in st st.

Rows 10 and 11: Knit.

Beg with a p row, work a further 7 rows in st st.

Row 19: (K1, inc1) 4 times (12 sts).

Row 20: Purl.

Row 21: (K2, inc1) 4 times (16 sts).

Row 22: Purl.

Row 23: (K3, inc1) 4 times (20 sts).

Row 24: Purl.

Row 25: (K4, inc1) 4 times (24 sts).

Row 26: Purl.

Row 27: (K3, inc1) 6 times (30 sts).

Row 28: Purl.

Cast off.

Feet (make 4)

Using 3.25mm needles and D, cast on 8 sts; cast off 4 sts; *transfer st from RH to LH needle, cast on 3 sts, cast off 4; rep from * twice more (4 toes); fasten off.

Making up

Body

Stuff body, then pull up tail of yarn at neck end and fasten off, closing gap. Use tail of yarn at other end of body to shape tail.

Head

Thread tail of yarn through all sts on cast-on edge and pull up to gather and shape nose and mouth; do not cut tail of yarn but leave for further shaping.

Face

Turn head inside out and stitch the seam along the underside of the chin. Attach eyes. Turn right sides out and begin to stitch opening to top front of body. Stuff firmly and finish stitching in place. On chin, pull the gathered cast-on edge under chin and stitch to seam, a few rows along, to further shape chin and mouth. Embroider nose and mouth using satin stitch and straight stitches. Stitch ears to sides of head.

Tuft

Make a bundle of yarn C and stitch to top of head; trim to form a tuft.

Whiskers

Insert lengths of nylon thread to form whiskers and add a few discreet stitches in the centre, to secure. (Note: you may wish to add a small blob of glue to the centre of each whisker before inserting through the snout, to hold firmly in place.)

Legs

To make up each leg, fold to inside along garter-stitch ridge then stitch seam. Stitch to body, stuffing as you do so. Use tails of yarn to shape toes, oversewing the edges of each one to make them thinner and firmer, then stitch feet to legs.

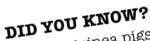

guinea pig

DID YOU KNOW?

In Peru, guinea pigs are kept for their meat.

Hamsters like to live indoors where it's warm, and they need plenty of activities in their cage to keep them busy. They love to climb, swing from the bars, and whizz around in the exercise wheel. Dwarf hamsters like a companion, but golden hamsters should be housed alone.

HAMSTER

DID YOU KNOW? Hamsters need their exercise. In the wild, they sometimes run up to 5 miles (8km) a day looking for food.

hamster

Information you'll need

Finished size
Hamster measures approximately
7in (18cm) long.

Materials
King Cole Merino Blend DK yarn 100%
pure new wool (123yds/112m per 50g ball)
1 x 50g ball in shade 790 Caramel (A)
1 x 50g ball in shade 1 White (B)
Small amount of pink 4-ply yarn
Set of four 3.25mm (UK10:US3)
double-pointed needles
1 pair of 3.25mm (UK10:US3) needles
Tapestry needle
Polyester toy filling
2 x round black beads
Sewing needle and black thread

Tension
24 sts and 34 rows to 4in (10cm),
measured over st st, using 3.25mm
needles. Use larger or smaller needles
if necessary to obtain correct tension.

Q: Where do hamsters go on holiday?
A: Hamsterdam!

How to make Hamster

Body (in one piece)

Using four 3.25mm double-pointed needles and A, cast on 3 sts and distribute between three needles.

Round 1: Knit.
Round 2: (Inc1) 3 times (6 sts).
Round 3: (Inc1) 6 times (12 sts).
Round 4: Knit.
Round 5: (K1, inc1) 6 times (18 sts).
Round 6: Knit.
Round 7: (K2, inc1) 6 times (24 sts).
Round 8: Knit.
Round 9: (K3, inc1) 6 times (30 sts).
Round 10: (Inc1, k4) twice, (k4, inc1) twice, k10 (34 sts).
Round 11: Knit.
Round 12: (Inc1, k5) twice, (k5, inc1) twice, k10 (38 sts).
Round 13: Knit.
Round 14: (Inc1, k6) twice, (k6, inc1) twice, k10 (42 sts).

Knit 13 rounds. Cut A and join in B.
Knit 8 rounds. Cut B and join in A.
Knit 3 rounds.

Shape front

Row 1: K8; turn.
Row 2: P26; turn.
Row 3: K25; turn.
Row 4: P24; turn.
Row 5: K23; turn.
Row 6: P22; turn.
Row 7: K21; turn.
Row 8: P20; turn and k15.

Shape neck

Round 1: (K5, k2tog) 6 times (36 sts).
Round 2: Knit.
Round 3: (K4, k2tog) 6 times (30 sts).
Round 4: Knit.
Round 5: (K3, k2tog) 6 times (24 sts).
Round 6: Knit.

Round 7: (K3, inc1) 6 times (30 sts).
Knit 2 rounds.
Round 10: (K3, k2tog) twice, k5, (k2tog, k3) twice, k5 (26 sts).
Knit 2 rounds.
Round 13: (K2, k2tog) twice, k5, (k2tog, k2) twice, k5 (22 sts).

Shape head

Row 1: K15; turn.
Row 2: P14; turn.
Row 3: K13; turn.
Row 4: P12; turn.
Row 5: K11; turn.
Row 6: P10; turn and k19; do not turn but resume working in rounds.
Next round: (K2, k2tog) twice, k2, (k2tog, k2) twice, k4 (18 sts).
Knit 4 rounds.
Next round: (K1, k2tog) 6 times (12 sts).
Next round: (K2tog) 6 times.
Cut yarn and thread through rem 6 sts.

Legs (make 4)

Using two 3.25mm double-pointed needles and B, cast on 4 sts.

Row 1: K4; do not turn but slide sts to other end of needle.

Rep row 1 four times.

Row 6: (K1, inc1) twice (6 sts); cut B; turn and join in A.

Row 7: Purl.

Row 8: (Inc1) 6 times (12 sts).

Row 9: Purl.

Row 10: (K2, inc1) 4 times (16 sts).

Row 11: Purl.

Cast off.

Ears (make 2)

Using 3.25mm needles and A, cast on 3 sts.

Row 1: Knit each st tbl.

Row 2: Purl.

Row 3: K1, inc1, k1 (4 sts).

Row 4: Purl.

Row 5: K1, (inc1) twice, k1 (6 sts).

Beg with a p row, work 3 rows in st st.

Row 9: K1, sl1, psso, k2tog, k1 (4 sts).

Row 10: Purl.

Row 11: K1, k2tog, k1 (3 sts).

Row 12: Purl.

Row 13: Sl1, k2tog, psso; cut yarn and fasten off.

Making up

Body and head

Stuff body and head, then pull up tail of yarn at head end and fasten off, closing gap; use tail of yarn to shape mouth and chin. Sew a running stitch around neck and pull up slightly to shape neck and back of head; fasten off securely.

Legs and ears

Stitch leg seams using mattress stitch and add a small amount of stuffing, or stuff with yarn ends, then sew cast-off edges to body. On each ear, run tail of yarn down one side and pull up, to shape ear, then sew this edge to head. Pinch top of each ear and use two or three small stitches to encourage it into a pointed shape.

Nose, mouth and claws

With pink yarn, embroider nose in satin stitch, then embroider one fly stitch to denote mouth. Use the same pink yarn to create small claws on each foot, using bullion stitch.

Eyes and tail

Stitch beads in place for eyes, taking thread right through head and pulling slightly so that eyes are slightly indented into the knitted fabric. Using yarn A, create a small tail using bullion stitch.

DID YOU KNOW?
'Hamstern' means 'hoard' in German. Hamsters can hoard extra food in their pouches.

hamster

Mice are sociable little animals, and should be housed with others of the same sex in a large, comfortable cage. They like to munch on seeds, grains and nuts. Mice are busy creatures that love to play on ropes and seesaws. They are active at dusk and dawn and during the night.

MOUSE

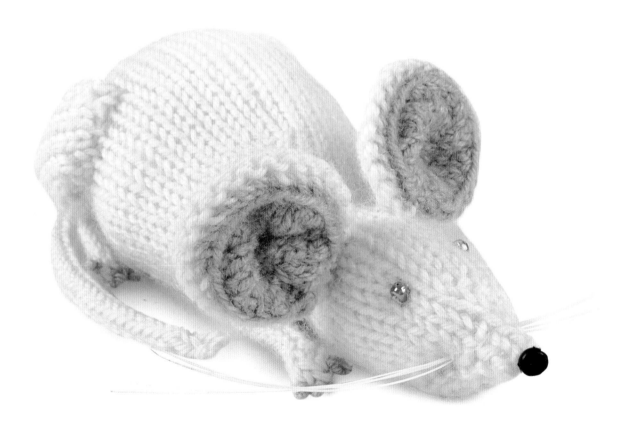

DID YOU KNOW?
A baby mouse is called a kitten or a pinky.

Information you'll need

Finished size
Mouse measures approximately 7½in (19cm) long, from nose to base of tail; tail measures approximately 6in (15cm).

Materials
King Cole Merino Blend DK 100% pure new wool (123yds/112m per 50g ball)
1 x 50g ball in shade 1 White (A)
Small amount of 4-ply yarn in dusty pink (B)
Set of four 3.25mm (UK10:US3) double-pointed needles
1 pair of 3.25mm (UK10:US3) needles
1 pair of 2.75mm (UK12:US2) needles
Tapestry needle
Polyester toy filling
2 pink seed beads
1 small black bead
White or translucent nylon thread for whiskers

Tension
23 sts and 30 rows to 4in (10cm) measured over st st, using 3.25mm needles. Use larger or smaller needles if necessary to obtain correct tension.

mouse

DID YOU KNOW?
A mouse's tail is the same length as its body.

How to make Mouse

Head, body and tail (in one piece)

Using two 3.25mm double-pointed needles and A, cast on 2 sts.

Row 1: Knit.
Row 2: Purl.
Row 3: Inc1 in each st (4 sts).
Row 4: Purl.
Row 5: Inc1, k2, inc1 (6 sts).
Row 6: Purl.
Row 7: (K1, inc1) 3 times (9 sts).

Divide sts between three double-pointed needles and, using the fourth needle to knit, begin working in rounds.

Round 1: Knit.
Round 2: (K2, inc1) 3 times (12 sts)
Round 3: (K3, inc1) 3 times (15 sts).
Round 4: (K4, inc1) 3 times (18 sts).
Round 5: (K5, inc1) 3 times (21 sts).
Knit 10 rounds.
Round 16: (K2tog, k5) 3 times (18 sts).
Round 17: Knit.
Round 18: (K1, k2tog) 6 times (12 sts).
Round 19: Knit.
Round 20: (Inc1, k3) 3 times (15 sts).
Round 21: (Inc1, k4) 3 times (18 sts).
Round 22: (Inc1, k5) 3 times (21 sts).

Round 23: (Inc1, k6) 3 times (24 sts).
Round 24: (Inc1, k7) 3 times (27 sts).
Round 25: (Inc1, k8) 3 times (30 sts).
Round 26: (Inc1, k9) 3 times (33 sts).
Round 27: (Inc1, k10) 3 times (36 sts).
Knit 12 rounds.
Round 40: (K4, k2tog) 6 times (30 sts).
Round 41: Knit.
Round 42: (K3, k2tog) 6 times (24 sts).
Round 43: (K2, k2tog) 6 times (18 sts).
Round 44: (K1, k2tog) 6 times (12 sts).
Round 45: (K2tog) 6 times (6 sts).
Round 46: (K2tog) 3 times (3 sts).

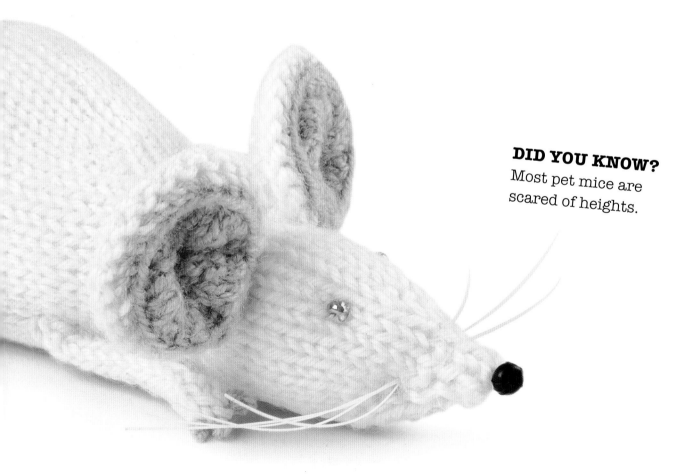

DID YOU KNOW?

Most pet mice are scared of heights.

Tail

Using only two double-pointed needles, k3; do not turn but slide sts to other end of needle.

Rep last row until tail is desired length; fasten off.

Front legs (make two)

Using two double-pointed needles and A, cast on 3 sts.

Row 1: K3; do not turn but slide sts to other end of needle.

Rep row 1 13 times; turn.

Row 14: Purl.

Cut yarn, leaving a long tail, and thread through all sts.

Back legs

Using two double-pointed needles and A, cast on 3 sts.

Row 1: K3; do not turn but slide sts to other end of needle.

Rep row 1 13 times; turn.

Row 14: Purl.

Row 15 (RS): Inc1, k to last st, inc1 (5 sts).

Row 16: Purl.

Rep rows 15 and 16 until there are 11sts, ending with RS facing.

Beg with a k row, work 4 rows in st st.

Dec 1 st at each end of next and each alt RS (knit) row until 5 sts rem.

Next row: Purl.

Cast off, leaving a tail of yarn.

Ears (make 2)

Using 3.25mm needles and A, cast on 1 st.

Row 1: Inc2 (knit into the front, back and front of st) (3 sts).

Row 2 (and each WS row): Purl.

Row 3: (Inc1) 3 times (6 sts).

Row 5: (Inc1) 6 times (12 sts).

Row 7: (K1, inc1) 6 times (18 sts).

Row 9: (K2, inc1) 6 times (24 sts).

Row 10: Purl.

Cast off knitwise, knitting each st tbl.

Ear linings (make 2)

Using 2.75mm knitting needles and B, follow instructions for ears.

Making up
Head and body

Stuff the body and head quite firmly and use tails of yarn to sew up openings.

Legs

On back legs, thread the tail of yarn in a tapestry needle, stitch a running stitch around the flat part of the knitted shape and pull up slightly. Then stitch one back leg to each side of the body, adding padding as you go. Stitch front legs in place.

Ears

Stitch ear linings inside ears, then gather lower edge of each ear to create a curved shape and stitch in place on top of head.

Facial features

Insert whiskers and add a few discreet stitches in the centre, to secure. (Note: you may wish to add a small blob of glue to the centre of each whisker before inserting through the nose, to hold firmly in place.) Stitch beads in place for eyes and nose.

If you are making this pet for a very young child, omit the whiskers and beads and embroider the eyes and nose instead.

mouse

Tarantulas are large and hairy, and look scary. But they are quiet pets that need little space and are easy to care for. A tarantula will be content in a terrarium with a soil floor, a hide area and a heating pad to keep it cosy. It likes to eat well-fed crickets.

TARANTULA

Information you'll need

Finished size
Tarantula's body measures approximately 5½in (14cm) long.

Materials
Rowan Cashsoft DK, 57% extra fine merino, 33% acrylic microfibre, 10% cashmere (126yds/115m per 50g ball)
1 x 50g ball in shade 519 Black (A)
Rowan Amy Butler Belle Organic DK, 50% organic cotton, 50% wool (131yds/120m per 50g ball)
1 x 50g ball in shade 07 Burnt Orange (B)
Set of four 3mm (UK11:US2–3) double-pointed needles
1 pair of 3mm (UK11:US2–3) needles
Tapestry needle
Polyester toy filling
4 x 10in (25cm) chenille sticks (thick pipe cleaners)
Wire brush or teasel

Important note: This knitted pet is not suitable for small children, due to the wire in the pipe cleaners.

Tension
22 sts and 32 rows to 4in (10cm), measured over st st, using 3mm needles. Use larger or smaller needles if necessary to obtain correct tension.

DID YOU KNOW?
A tarantula bites! Its bite feels like a bee sting and may throb and ache.

How to make Tarantula

Body and head (in one piece)

Using four 3mm double-pointed needles and A, cast on 3 sts and distribute between three needles.

Round 1: Inc1 in each st (6 sts).
Round 2: Inc1 in each st (12 sts).
Round 3: Knit.
Round 4: (K1, inc1) 6 times (18 sts).
Round 5: Knit.
Round 6: (K2, inc1) 6 times (24 sts).
Round 7: Knit.
Round 8: (K3, inc1) 6 times (30 sts).
Round 9: Knit.
Round 10: (K4, inc1) 6 times (36 sts).

Round 11: Knit.
Round 12: (K5, inc1) 6 times (42 sts).
Knit 8 rounds.
Round 21: (K5, sl1, k1, psso) 6 times (36 sts).
Round 22: Knit.
Round 23: (K4, sl1, k1, psso) 6 times (30 sts).
Round 24: Knit.
Round 25: (K3, sl1, k1, psso) 6 times (24 sts).
Round 26: Knit.
Round 27: (K2, sl1, k1, psso) 6 times (18 sts).
Round 28: Knit.
Round 29: (K1, sl1, k1, psso) 6 times (12 sts); do not cut yarn A but join in B.
Round 30: Using B, (k1, inc1) 6 times (18 sts).

Round 31: Knit; cut yarn B.
Round 32: Using A, (k2, inc1) 6 times (24 sts).
Knit 3 rounds.
Round 36: (K3, inc1) 6 times (30 sts).
Round 37: Knit.
Round 38: (K4, inc1) 6 times (36 sts); cut yarn A and rejoin B.
Knit 3 rounds.
Round 42: (K4, sl1, k1, psso) 6 times (30 sts).
Round 43: Knit.
Round 44: (K3, sl1, k1, psso) 6 times (24 sts).
Round 45: Knit.
Round 46: (K2, sl1, k1, psso) 6 times (18 sts).
Round 47: (K1, sl1, k1, psso) 6 times (12 sts); cut yarn B and rejoin A.
Round 48: Using A, k5, *inc2 in next st, k1, turn, p5, turn, k5, turn, p5, turn, k1, k3tog, k4, rep from * once more, k4.
Round 49: Knit.
Round 50: (K2tog) 6 times (6 sts).
Cut yarn and thread through rem sts.

Legs (make 8)

Using 3mm needles and B, cast on 7 sts.
Row 1: K each st tbl.
Row 2: Purl; do not cut B but join in A.
Continuing in st st, work the following, drawing the yarn not in use up the side of your work:
10 rows in A.
8 rows in B.
4 rows in A.
4 rows in B.
2 rows in A.
2 rows in B; cut yarn.
4 rows in A; cut yarn, leaving a tail, and thread through all sts.

Feelers (make 2)

Using 3mm needles and A, cast on 7 sts.
Row 1: K each st tbl.
Row 2: Purl; cut A and join in B.
Using B, and beg with a k row, work 8 rows in st st; cut yarn and thread through all sts.

Making up

Body

Stuff body and pull up tail of yarn to close gap. Thread this tail into a tapestry needle and stitch a running stitch around each bobble to exaggerate the shape and create a pair of jaws. On each feeler, overlap side edges and stitch firmly to form tight tubes, then stitch firmly to front of body, one each side of the jaws.

Legs

Fold each leg in half, with right sides together. Pull up tail of yarn at foot end and use this yarn to stitch a neat backstitch seam, leaving cast-on edge open. Turn right sides out. Cut each pipe cleaner in half and fold over approx. ½in (12mm) at each end, twisting to secure. Then insert half a prepared pipe cleaner into each leg and, with four legs on each side of cephalothorax (front body), stitch open end of leg in place.

Use a wire brush or teasel to brush the centre part of each leg downwards towards foot, then bend each leg downwards at this point and upwards just above feet.

Fangs very much for knitting me.

DID YOU KNOW?
The giant Goliath tarantula has a leg span of 1ft (30cm) and its fangs are 1in (2.5cm) long.

Budgerigars, or budgies, are colourful, friendly birds that can live for up to 15 years. They can be kept in an outdoor aviary or a large indoor cage. Indoor budgies should be let out every day for exercise, but keep the windows closed so they can't escape.

BUDGIE

Information you'll need

Finished size
Budgie measures 7in (18cm) long and 3in (8cm) wide.

Materials
Millamia Naturally Soft Merino DK (137yds/125m per 50g ball)
1 x 50g ball in shade 142 Daisy Yellow (A)
1 x 50g ball in shade 141 Grass (B)
1 x 50g ball in shade 144 Peacock (C)
Small amount of DK yarn in pink (D), acid yellow (E), black and blue
Set of four 3mm (UK11:US2–3) double-pointed needles
1 pair of 3mm (UK11:US2–3) needles
Tapestry needle
Polyester toy filling
Thick, flexible plastic sheet – use the lid of a food container, or buy a small sheet of polypropylene from a stationery supplier

Tension
24 sts and 32 rows to 4in (10cm), measured over st st, using 3mm needles. Use larger or smaller needles if necessary to obtain correct tension.

budgie

How to make Budgie

Head, body and tail (in one piece)

Using set of four 3mm double-pointed needles and A, cast on 3 sts and divide between three needles.

Round 1: Inc1 in each st (6 sts).
Round 2: Inc1 in each st (12 sts).
Round 3: Knit.
Round 4: (K1, inc1) 6 times (18 sts).
Round 5: Knit.
Round 6: (K2, inc1) 6 times (24 sts).
Knit 5 rounds.
Round 12: (K3, inc1) 6 times (30 sts).
Knit 2 rounds.
Round 15: K1, join in B and k1B, *k1A, k1B; rep from * to end of round; cut yarn A.
Round 16: Knit.
Round 17: (K4, inc1) 6 times (36 sts).
Round 18: Knit.
Round 19: K13, (inc1, k2) 3 times, inc1, k13 (40 sts).
Knit 5 rounds.
Round 25: K13, (k2tog, k2) 3 times, k2tog, k13 (36 sts).
Knit 3 rounds.
Round 29: (K4, k2tog) 6 times (30 sts).
Knit 5 rounds.
Round 35: (K3, k2tog) 6 times (24 sts).
Knit 5 rounds.
Round 41: (K2, k2tog) 6 times (18 sts).
Knit 1 round.
Round 43: K5, (k2tog) 4 times, k5 (14 sts).
Round 44: K5, (k2tog) twice, k5 (12 sts).

Tail (worked in rows)

Row 1: K4; turn.
Row 2: P8, turn and leave rem sts on a holder; continue using only two needles.
Row 3: Cast on 4 sts, k to end (12 sts).
Row 4: Cast on 4 sts, p to end (16 sts).
Beg with a k row, work 6 rows in st st.
Row 11: K1, sl1, k1, psso, k10, k2tog, k1 (14 sts).
Beg with a p row, work 5 rows in st st.

Row 17: K1, sl1, k1, psso, k8, k2tog, k1 (12 sts).
Row 18: Purl; cut B and join in C.
Beg with a k row, using C, work 6 rows in st st.
Row 25: K1, sl1, k1, psso, k6, k2tog, k1 (10 sts).
Beg with a p row, work 7 rows in st st.
Cast off.

Wings (make 2)

Using 3mm needles and A, cast on 5 sts.
Row 1: Purl.
Row 2: (K1, inc1) twice, k1 (7 sts).
Row 3: Purl.
Row 4: K1, inc1, k1, inc2, k1, inc1, k1 (11 sts).
Row 5: Purl.
Row 6: K1, inc1, k3, inc2, k3, inc1, k1 (15 sts).
Beg with a p row, work 3 rows in st st.
Row 10: K1, inc1, k5, inc2, k5, inc1, k1 (19 sts).
Beg with a p row, work 3 rows in st st.
Row 14: K1, inc1, k7, inc2, k7, inc1, k1 (23 sts).
Beg with a p row, work 5 rows in st st.
Row 20: K1, sl1, k1, psso, k to last 3 sts, k2tog, k1.
Row 21: Purl.
Rep rows 20 and 21 until 15 sts remain.
Row 28: K1, sl1, k1, psso, k3, sl1, k2tog, psso, k3, k2tog, k1 (11 sts).
Row 29: Purl.
Row 30: K1, sl1, k1, psso, k to last 3 sts, k2tog, k1.
Rep rows 29 and 30 once more (7 sts).
Beg with a p row, work 7 rows in st st.
Cast off.

DID YOU KNOW?

Budgies poo every 15 minutes or so.

Feet (make 6)

Using two 3mm double-pointed needles and D, cast on 2 sts.
Row 1: K2; do not turn but slide sts to other end of needle.
Rep row 1 nine times more.
Cast off.

Beak

Using 3mm needles and E, cast on 1 st.
Row 1: Knit.
Row 2: Inc2 knitwise (3 sts).
Row 3: Purl.
Row 4: Inc1, k1, inc1 (5 sts); cut yarn E and join in C.
Row 5: Using C, inc1, p5, inc1 (7 sts).
Cut yarn, leaving a tail, and thread through all sts.

Making up

Head and body

Stuff head and body. Cut a strip of plastic ¾in (2cm) x 4in (10cm) and shape one end into a curved point. Slip the pointed end into the tail and the other end up into the body, towards the back.

Tail

Using tail of yarn, stitch tail seam, then sew a running stitch through all stitches at top of tail and through 4 stitches on holder. Push a few wisps of stuffing into top part of tail, then pull up yarn and fasten off, closing the hole.

Wings

Fold each wing in half and stitch sides together, adding a few wisps of stuffing. Stitch wings to sides of body, with wing tips towards back of tail.

Head

Using matching yarn, sew a running stitch around base of head and pull up to shape neck. Stitch beak in place at front of head.

Embroidery

Using black yarn and Swiss darning, embroider individual stitches, evenly spaced all over wings, then straight stitches at wing tips, using picture of finished bird as a guide. Still using black, embroider running stitches in rows across back of head, two satin stitch eyes and two pairs of straight stitches below beak, on either side. Using blue, embroider two small cheek patches on either side of beak.

Feet

Stitch both ends of feet pieces to underside of body, wrapping each one around a stick, to make a perch.

budgie

He wouldn't budgie so I just had to move him.

Parrots are lively, interesting pets to keep. But note that some kinds live so long that they could be with you all your life! A large parrot cage makes a good home, but let your parrot out every day to stretch his or her wings. Parrots enjoy a varied diet of different fruits, seeds and vegetables.

PARROT

Information you'll need

Finished size
Parrot measures approximately 13½in (34cm) from the top of her head to the tip of her tail.

Materials
King Cole Merino Blend DK yarn 100% pure new wool (123yds/112m per 50g ball)
1 x 50g ball in shade 9 Scarlet (A)
1 x 50g ball in shade 1 White (B)
1 x 50g ball in shade 18 Turquoise (C)
1 x 50g ball in shade 55 Gold (D)
Small amount in shade 702 Graphite (F)
King Cole Pricewise DK yarn 100% acrylic (310yds/282m per 100g ball)
Small amount in shade 48 Black (E)
Set of four 3mm (UK11:US2–3) double-pointed needles
1 pair of 3mm (UK11:US2–3) needles
Tapestry needle
Polyester toy filling
2 x ½in (12mm) blue safety eyes
Thin grey or black pipe cleaner, 12in (30cm) long
Thick, flexible plastic sheet – use the lid of a food container, or buy a small sheet of polypropylene from a stationery supplier

Tension
24 sts and 32 rows to 4in (10cm), measured over st st, using 3mm needles. Use larger or smaller needles if necessary to obtain correct tension.

Learn to knit parrot-fashion!

parrot

DID YOU KNOW?
Parrots brought up in a household where two languages are spoken become bilingual themselves!

How to make Parrot

Tail, body, head and beak (in one piece, beginning at tail)

Using set of four 3mm double-pointed needles and A, cast on 6 sts and divide between three needles.

Knit 3 rounds.

Round 4: Inc1 in each st (12 sts).

Knit 36 rounds.

Round 41: (Inc1, k3) 3 times (15 sts).

Knit 7 rounds.

Round 49: (Inc1, k4) 3 times (18 sts).

Knit 2 rounds.

Round 52: K12, inc1, k4, inc1 (20 sts).

Round 53: Knit.

Round 54: K12, inc1, k6, inc1 (22 sts).

Round 55: Knit.

Round 56: K12, inc1, k8, inc1 (24 sts).

Round 57: Knit.

Round 58: K12, inc1, k10, inc1 (26 sts).

Round 59: Knit.

Round 60: K12, inc1, k12, inc1 (28 sts).

Round 61: Knit.

Round 62: K12, inc1, k14, inc1 (30 sts).

Round 63: Knit.

Round 64: K12, inc1, k16, inc1 (32 sts).

Round 65: Knit.

Round 66: K12, inc1, k5, inc1, k6, inc1, k5, inc 1 (36 sts).

Knit 5 rounds.

Round 72: K12, inc1, k6, inc1, k8, inc1, k6, inc 1 (40 sts).

Knit 4 rounds.

Round 77: K12, inc1, k26, inc1 (42 sts).

Knit 4 rounds.

Round 82: K12, inc1, k28, inc1 (44 sts).

Knit 16 rounds.

Round 99: K12, k2tog, k28, k2tog (42 sts).

Round 100: Knit.

Round 101: K12, k2tog, k26, k2tog (40 sts).

Round 102: Knit.

Round 103: K12, k2tog, k24, k2tog (38 sts).

Round 104: Knit.

Round 105: K12, k2tog, k22, k2tog (36 sts).

Round 106: Knit.

Round 107: K12, k2tog, k20, k2tog (34 sts).

Round 108: K12, k2tog, k18, k2tog (32 sts).

Round 109: Knit.

Round 110: K12, k2tog, k16, k2tog (30 sts).

Shape head (working in rows)

Row 1: K19, turn.

Row 2: P26, turn.

Row 3: K25, turn.

Row 4: P24, turn.

Row 5: K23, turn.

Row 6: P22, turn.

Row 7: K21, turn.

Row 8: P20, turn.

Row 9: K19, turn.

Row 10: P18, turn.

Row 11: K17, turn.

Row 12: P16, turn.

Row 13: K15, turn.

Row 14: P14, turn.

Row 15: K13, turn.

Row 16: P12, turn.

Row 17: K11, turn.

Row 18: P10, turn.

Row 19: K9, turn.

Row 20: P20, turn.

Row 21: K30; do not turn.

Row 22: Cast off 9 sts, k20 (there are 21 sts on needle), turn and cast off 9 sts purlwise, p to end (12 sts).

Knit 1 row and purl 1 row; cut yarn A and join in B.

Upper beak (worked in rows on 2 needles)

Row 1: Cast on 4 sts, k to end (16 sts).

Row 2: Cast on 4 sts, p to end (20 sts).

Row 3: K4, sl1, k1, psso, k8, k2tog, k4 (18 sts).

Row 4: Purl.

Row 5: K4, sl1, k1, psso, k6, k2tog, k4 (16 sts).

Row 6: Purl.

Row 7: K4, sl1, k1, psso, k4, k2tog, k4 (14 sts).

Row 8: Purl.

Row 9: K4, sl1, k1, psso, k2, k2tog, k4 (12 sts).

Row 10: Purl.

Row 11: (K1, sl1, k1, psso) twice, (k2tog, k1) twice (8 sts).

Row 12: P1, p2tog, p2, p2tog, p1 (6 sts).

Row 13: K1, sl1, k1, psso, k2tog, k1 (4 sts).

Row 14: Purl

Row 15: Knit.

Row 16: Purl.

Cast off.

Lower beak

Using 3mm needles and yarn E, pick up and knit 12 sts from lower edge of head opening.

Row 1: Cast on 6 sts, p to end (18 sts).

Row 2: Cast on 6 sts, (k2, k2tog) 6 times (18 sts).

Row 3: Purl.

Row 4: (K1, k2tog) 6 times (12 sts).

Row 5: Purl.

Row 6: (K2tog) 6 times (6 sts).

Row 7: (P2tog) 3 times (3 sts).

Row 8: Sl1, k2tog, psso; fasten off.

Eye patches (make 2)

Using 3mm needles and yarn B, cast on
1 st.

Row 1: Inc2 (3 sts).
Rows 2 and 3: Knit.
Row 4: K1, inc1, k1 (4 sts).
Row 5: Knit.
Row 6: K1, inc1, k to end.
Rep rows 5 and 6 six times more (11 sts).
Knit 3 rows.
Cast off.

Wings (make 2)

Using 3mm needles and C, cast on 3 sts.
Row 1: Inc1 in each st (6 sts).
Beg with a p row, work 3 rows in st st.
Row 5: K1, inc1, k2, inc1, k1 (8 sts).
Row 6: Purl.
Row 7: (K2, inc1) twice, k2, (10 sts).
Row 8: Purl.
Row 9: K2, inc1, k4, inc1, k2 (12 sts).
Beg with a p row, work 7 rows in st st.
Row 17: K1, inc1, k to last 3 sts, k2tog,
k1.
Row 18: Purl.
Rep rows 17 and 18 once more; cut C and
join in D.
Row 21: K1, inc1, k to last 2 sts, inc1, k1
(14 sts).
Beg with a p row, work 5 rows in st st.
Row 27: K1, inc1, k to last 2 sts, inc1, k1
(16 sts).
Row 28: P12, turn.
Row 29: K to end.
Row 30: P8, turn.
Row 31: K to end.
Beg with a p row, work 3 rows in st st; cut
D and join in A.

*What do you get if you
leave the cage door open?
Polygon!*

Beg with a k row, work 8 rows in st st.
Row 43: K1, sl1, k1, psso, k to last 3 sts,
k2tog, k1.
Row 44: Purl.
Rep rows 43 and 44 four times more
(6 sts).
Cut yarn and thread tail through rem 6 sts.
Work second wing, reversing shaping.

Single claws (make 2)

Using 3mm needles and yarn F, cast on
12 sts.
Row 1: Knit each st tbl.
Cast off, knitting each st tbl.

Double claws (make 2)

Using 3mm needles and yarn F, cast on
25 sts.
Row 1: Knit each st tbl.
Cast off, knitting each st tbl.

Making up
Head, body and tail

Cut a strip of plastic 1in (2.5cm) x 9in
(23cm) and shape one end into a curved
point. Slip the pointed end into the tail
and the other end up into the body,
towards the back. Stuff body. Stuff head,
to determine size and shape, then pin eye
patches in position on either side of head
and stitch firmly in place by oversewing
edges. Attach eyes and secure. Continue
adding stuffing to head and, at the same
time, stitch end of upper beak to form a
point, pulling on stitches to cause end of
beak to curve, then stitch lower beak to
underside of upper beak, adding more
stuffing as you do so. Ensure that head
and beak are firmly stuffed before last
stitches are made.

Wings

Stitch together the sides of the first few
rows at the tip of each wing to form a
point, then pin each wing in position to
sides of body, with wing tips towards back
of tail, and stitch in place, allowing the
sides to curl under slightly, and adding
a little stuffing as you go.

Claws

Cut six 2in (5cm) lengths of thin pipe
cleaner. Bend over 1⁄8in (3mm) at each end
of each piece of pipe cleaner, to prevent
wires from protruding. Place two of these
prepared pieces, end to end, inside each
double claw strip, then fold the strip over
to enclose and stitch cast-on and cast-
off edges together by oversewing. Place
one piece of pipe cleaner inside each
single claw strip, then fold the strip over
to enclose and stitch cast-on and cast-off
edges together by oversewing. To form
each claw, bend a double strip in half
and stitch one end of a single strip to the
centre fold, then oversew this join very
firmly. Stitch this join to the base of the
parrot's body and bend claws over so that
they can grip the perch.

parrot

93

Tortoises are not dull and slow – they're more fun than you think. If they're kept warm and well fed, tortoises are active and curious. They adore munching on wild plants and flowers. Tortoises are sun-loving creatures, but like a well-lit indoor home when the weather is bad.

TORTOISE

Information you'll need

Finished size
Tortoise body measures approximately 9½in (24cm) long and 8in (20cm) wide; shell measures 7in (18cm) long and 5in (12cm) wide.

Materials
Manos Maxima 100% extra-fine merino variegated yarn (219yds/200m per 100g twisted skein)
1 x 100g skein in shade 9201 Rocky Road (A)
Artesano Superwash Merino DK yarn 100% merino (120yds/112m per 50g ball)
1 x 50g ball in shade 7254 Sand Yellow (B)
1 x 50g ball in shade 6315 Lime Green (C)
1 pair of 3.75mm needles (UK9:US5)
1 pair of 4mm needles (UK8:US6)
Tapestry needle
Polyester toy filling
Pair of round black safety eyes
Press fasteners x 5

Tension
20 sts and 27 rows to 4in (10cm) measured over st st, using 4mm needles and yarn A. Use larger or smaller needles if necessary to obtain correct tension.

tortoise

DID YOU KNOW?
Two tortoises together will often nuzzle each other with affection.

How to make Tortoise

Upper shell

Using 4mm needles and A, cast on 10 sts.
*Row 1 (WS): Purl.
Row 2: K1, inc1, k to last 2 sts, inc1, k1.
Rep rows 1 and 2 until there are 28 sts.
Beg with a purl row, work 7 rows in st st.
Next row: K1, sl1, psso, k to last 3 sts, k2tog, k1.
Next row: Purl.
Rep last 2 rows until 10 sts rem, ending with RS facing.*
Next row: Purl (to create ridge).
Rep from * to * then cast off.

Under-shell
Left side

Using 3.75mm needles and B, cast on 8 sts.
Row 1: P to last 2 sts, k2.
Row 2: K to last 2 sts, inc1, k1.
Rep rows 1 and 2 until there are 19 sts.
Row 23: P to last 2 sts, k2.
Row 24: Knit.
Rep last 2 rows three times more.
Row 31: P to last 2 sts, k2.

Row 32: K to last 3 sts, k2tog, k1.
Rep rows 31 and 32 until 8 sts rem, ending with WS facing.
Knit 1 row.
Cast off.
Work right side to match, reversing shaping.

Head, body and tail base
(worked in one piece)

Using 3.75mm needles and C, cast on 4 sts.
Row 1: Purl.
Row 2: Inc1, k2, inc1 (6 sts).
Row 3: Purl.
Row 4: Inc1, k4, inc1 (8 sts).
Beg with a p row, work 7 rows in st st.
Row 12: K1, sl1, psso, k to last 3 sts, k2tog, k1 (6 sts).
Row 13: Purl.
Row 14: Knit.
Row 15: Purl.
Row 16: K1, inc1, k to last 2 sts, inc1, k1.
Rep rows 15 and 16 until there are 30 sts.
Work 5 rows in st st without shaping.
Row 44: K1, sl1, k1, psso, k to last 3 sts, k2tog, k1.

Row 45: Purl.
Rep rows 44 and 45 until 8 sts rem.
Row 66: K2tog, k4, k2tog (6 sts).
Beg with a p row, work 7 rows in st st.
Row 74: K1, sl1, k1, psso, k2tog, k1 (4 sts).
Row 75: Purl.
Row 76: K1, sl1, k1, psso, k1 (3 sts).
Row 77: Purl.
Row 78: Sl1, k2tog, psso; cut yarn and fasten off.

Head, body and tail top
(worked in one piece)

Follow instructions for Head, body and tail base to end of row 5.
Shape top of head
Row 6: K3, (inc1) twice, k3 (10 sts).
Row 7: Purl.
Row 8: K4, (inc1) twice, k4 (12 sts).
Row 9: Purl.
Row 10: K2, sl1, k2tog, psso, k3tog, k2 (8 sts).
Row 11: Purl.
Continue as for Base from row 12 to end.

Legs (make 8)

Using 3.75mm needles and C, cast on
4 sts.

Rows 1–3: Knit.
Row 4: Inc1, k to last st, inc1.
Rep rows 1–4 once more (8 sts).
Rows 9–11: Knit.
Row 12: K2, turn.
Row 13: K2.
Row 14: K3, turn.
Row 15: K3.
Row 16: K4, turn.
Row 17: K4.
Row 18: K5, turn.
Row 19: K5.
Row 20: K6, turn.
Row 21: K6.
Rows 22 and 23: Knit to end of row.
Row 24: Inc1, k to last st, inc1 (10 sts).
Rows 25–28: Knit.
Row 29: Inc1, k to last st, inc1 (12 sts).
Row 30: K2tog, k8, k2tog (10 sts).
Row 31: K2tog, k6, k2tog (8 sts).
Row 32: K2tog, k4, k2tog (6 sts).
Cast off.

Making up
Stitching shell

Thread tapestry needle with yarn B and
stitch lines of chain stitch on one half of
carapace (upper shell), to correspond with
the lines of embroidery in the photograph,
and following the lines of stitching. Begin
with a central shape, then stitch a ring of
chain stitches just inside the outer edges of
the shell. Join the two with lines of chain
stitch radiating out from the central shape.
Stitch the two upper shell pieces together
all round, stuffing lightly before closing up
the gap between the two.

Stitch the two halves of the plastron
(under-shell) to the top shell at the sides
and at the front and back corners, leaving
gaps for the head, tail and legs. Stitch
press fasteners to the garter stitch borders
on each half.

Stitching body together

On the top half of the body, fix eyes
in place at front of shaped head, then
stitch the two body pieces together,
stuffing quite firmly before closing up the
gap between the two. Stitch leg pieces
together on both sides, in four pairs.
Stuff each leg and oversew cast-off edges
together on each one, then stitch to
sloping sides of body.

tortoise

DID YOU KNOW?
The top of a tortoise's shell
is called a carapace and the
under-shell is a plastron.

97

Common goldfish can grow up to 8in (20cm) long and live for up to 20 years –
if you care for them well. A couple of goldfish will be content in a large 20-gallon (9-litre)
tank with rocks and plastic plants to create hiding places. You can feed them fish flakes
and throw in a few live shrimps for variety.

GOLDFISH

goldfish

Information you'll need

Finished size
Goldfish measures approximately
8in (20cm) long, including tail.

Materials
Anchor Tapestry wool
2 x 10m skeins in main colour (A)
2 x 10m skeins in contrast colour (B)
1 pair of 3mm (UK11:US2–3) needles
1 pair of 2.75mm (UK12:US2) needles
Tapestry needle
Polyester toy filling
2 blue sequins
2 white seed beads
Needle and sewing thread

Tension
24 sts and 32 rows to 4in (10cm)
measured over st st, using 3mm needles.
Use larger or smaller needles if necessary
to obtain correct tension.

DID YOU KNOW?
Goldfish can recognize
different human faces
and voices.

How to make Goldfish

Body (make 2)

Using 3mm needles and A, cast on 3 sts.
Row 1: Purl.
Row 2: Inc1, k1, inc1 (5 sts).
Row 3: Sl1 knitwise, p3, k1.
Row 4: Sl1, k4.
Row 5: Sl1 knitwise, p to last st, k1.
Row 6: Inc1, k3, inc1 (7 sts).
Row 7: Sl1 knitwise, p to last st, k1.
Row 8: Inc1, k5, inc1 (9 sts).
Row 9: Sl1 knitwise, p to last st, k1.
Row 10: K3, p3, k3.
Row 11: P4, k1, p4.
Row 12: Inc1, k3, p1, k3, inc1 (11 sts).
Row 13: Sl1, p to last st, k1.
Row 14: Sl1, k to end.
Row 15: Sl1, p to last st, k1.
Row 16: Inc1, k to last st, inc1.

Row 17: Sl1, p to last st, k1.
Rep rows 14–17 twice more (17 sts).
Row 26: Sl1, k to end.
Row 27: Sl1, p to last st, k1.
Rep rows 26 and 27 four times more.
Row 36: K2tog, k to last 2 sts, k2tog (15 sts).
Row 37: Sl1, p to last st, k1.
Row 38: Sl1, k to end.
Row 39: Sl1, p to last st, k1.
Row 40: K2tog, k to last 2 sts, k2tog.
Row 41: Sl1, p to last st, k1.
Rep rows 40 and 41 until 3 sts rem.
Next row: Sl1, k2tog, psso.
Cut yarn, leaving a long tail for sewing up; fasten off.
Stitch the two bodies together, stuffing as you go.

Tail

Using 2.75mm needles and yarn B, pick up and knit 6 sts at tail end (3 sts on each side).
Row 1: K2, (inc1) twice, k2 (8 sts).
Row 2: K3, (inc1) twice, k3 (10 sts).
Row 3: (K1, p1) twice, (inc1) twice, (k1, p1) twice (12 sts).
Row 4: (K1, p1) twice, k1 (inc1) twice, (p1, k1) twice, p1 (14 sts).
Row 5: (K1, p1) three times, (inc1) twice, (k1, p1) three times (16 sts).
Row 6: (K1, p1) three times, k1 (inc1) twice, (p1, k1) three times, p1 (18 sts).
Row 7: (K1, p1) four times, (inc1) twice, (k1, p1) four times (20 sts).
Row 8: (K1, p1) four times, k1 (inc1) twice, (p1, k1) four times, p1 (22 sts).
Row 9: (K1, p1) five times, (inc1) twice, (k1, p1) five times (24 sts).
Row 10 (divide): (K1, p1) six times, turn and leave rem sts on a spare needle.
Row 11: (K1, p1) six times.
Rep row 11 five times more.
Row 17: K2tog, (k1, p1) four times, k2tog (10 sts).
Row 18: K2tog, (p1, k1) three times, k2tog (8 sts).
Cast off in rib.
Work second half of tail to match.

DID YOU KNOW?
The world's oldest goldfish died peacefully in his bowl, aged 43.

Dorsal (top) fin

Using 2.75mm needles and yarn B, and beginning about halfway along back seam, pick up and knit 10 sts along back.

Row 1: (K1, p1) five times.

Row 2: (K1, p1) five times, then pick up and knit 1 st from seam (11 sts).

Row 3: (P1, k1) five times, p1.

Cont in this way, working in rib and picking up 1 extra st from back at end of next and each alt row until there are 15 sts.

Work 2 rows in rib then cast off in rib.

Pectoral and pelvic fins (make 4)

Using 2.75mm needles and yarn B, cast on 1 st.

Row 1: Inc2 (knit into front, back and front of st) (3 sts).

Row 2: K1, p1, k1.

Row 3: P1, k1, p1.

Row 4: Inc1, p1, inc1 (5 sts).

Row 5: (K1, p1) twice, k1.

Row 6: (P1, k1) twice, p1.

Row 7: Inc1, p1, k1, p1, inc1 (7 sts).

Row 8: (K1, p1) three times, k1.

Row 9: (P1, k1) three times, p1.

Row 10: Inc1, rib to last st, inc1 (9 sts).

Work 1 more row in rib then cast off in rib.

Making up

Using tails of yarn, stitch the fins in place using the photograph of the finished fish as a guide. Weave in all yarn ends. Using sewing needle and thread, stitch a sequin on each side of head to form eyes, holding each sequin in place with a small white bead.

goldfish

Iguanas come from hot, tropical countries, so a pet iguana needs to live in a warm, humid environment. These scaly reptiles eat leaves, which they swallow whole without chewing. Iguanas are cute when they are little but can grow to 6ft (1.8m) long. As adults, they may need a whole room to themselves!

IGUANA

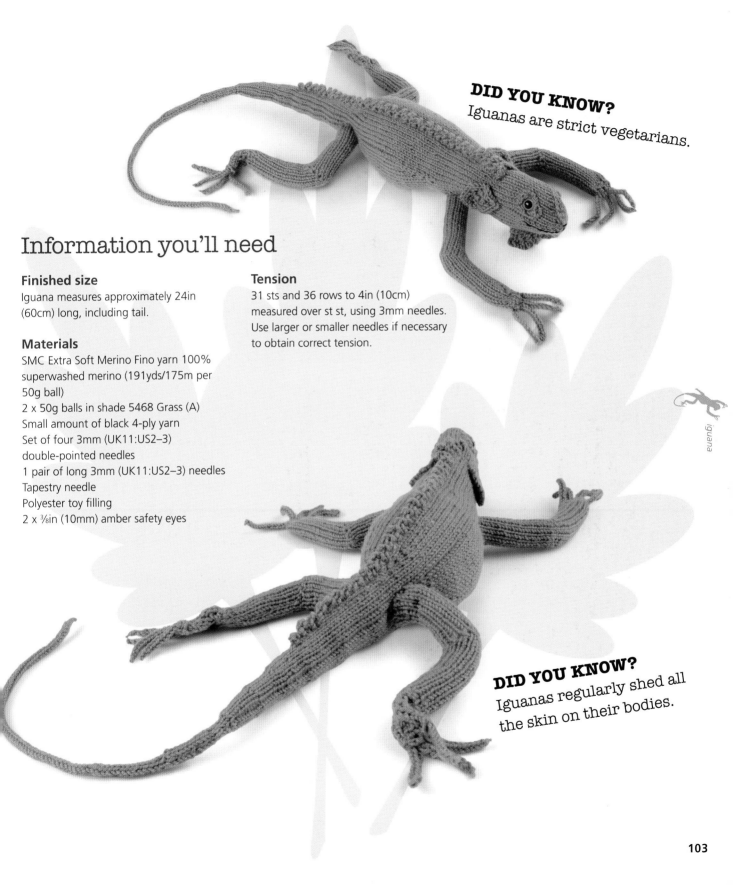

Information you'll need

Finished size
Iguana measures approximately 24in (60cm) long, including tail.

Materials
SMC Extra Soft Merino Fino yarn 100% superwashed merino (191yds/175m per 50g ball)
2 x 50g balls in shade 5468 Grass (A)
Small amount of black 4-ply yarn
Set of four 3mm (UK11:US2–3) double-pointed needles
1 pair of long 3mm (UK11:US2–3) needles
Tapestry needle
Polyester toy filling
2 x ⅜in (10mm) amber safety eyes

Tension
31 sts and 36 rows to 4in (10cm) measured over st st, using 3mm needles. Use larger or smaller needles if necessary to obtain correct tension.

iguana

DID YOU KNOW?
Iguanas regularly shed all the skin on their bodies.

How to make Iguana

Tail, body and head (in one piece)

Using two 3mm double-pointed needles and A, cast on 3 sts.

Row 1: K3; do not turn but slide sts to other end of needle.

Rep row 1 69 times more.

Row 71: K1, m1, k2 (4 sts).

Row 72: K4; do not turn but slide sts to other end of needle.

Rep row 72 14 times more.

Row 87: K1, m1, k1, m1, k2 (6 sts); distribute these sts between 3 needles and use fourth needle to knit in rounds.
Knit 15 rounds.

Round 16: (K1, inc1) 3 times (9 sts).
Knit 10 rounds

Round 27: (K2, inc1) 3 times (12 sts).
Knit 10 rounds.

Round 38: (K3, inc 1) 3 times (15 sts).
Knit 10 rounds.

Round 49: (K4, inc1) 3 times (18 sts).
Knit 10 rounds.

Begin stuffing tail and body, continuing to add more stuffing after every 10 rounds or so as work progresses.

Round 60: (K5, inc1) 3 times (21 sts).
Knit 10 rounds.

Round 71: (K6, inc1) 3 times (24 sts).
Knit 10 rounds.

Round 82: (K3, inc1) 6 times (30 sts).
Knit 2 rounds.

Round 85: (K4, inc1) 6 times (36 sts).
Knit 2 rounds.

Round 88: (K5, inc1) 6 times (42 sts).
Knit 2 rounds.

Round 91: K14, (inc1, k6) 4 times (46 sts).
Knit 1 round.

Round 93: K14, (inc1, k7) 4 times (50 sts).
Knit 1 round.

Round 95: K14, (inc1, k8) 4 times (54 sts).
Knit 14 rounds.

Round 110: K14, (sl1, k1, psso, k8) twice, (k8, k2tog) twice (50 sts).
Knit 2 rounds.

Round 113: K14, (sl1, k1, psso, k7) twice, (k7, k2tog) twice (46 sts).
Knit 2 rounds.

Round 116: K14, (sl1, k1, psso, k6) twice, (k6, k2tog) twice (42 sts).
Knit 2 rounds.

Round 119: (K5, k2tog) 6 times (36 sts).
Knit 18 rounds

Round 138: (K2tog, k4) 6 times (30 sts).
Knit 2 rounds.

Round 141: (K3, k2tog) 6 times (24 sts).
Knit 1 round.

Round 143: (K3, inc1) 6 times (30 sts).
Knit 11 rounds.

Round 155: (K8, k2tog) 3 times (27 sts).
Knit 1 round.

Round 157: (K7, k2tog) 3 times (24 sts).
Knit 1 round.

Round 159: (K6, k2tog) 3 times (21 sts).
Knit 1 round.

Round 161: (K5, k2tog) 3 times (18 sts).
Knit 1 round.

Round 163: (K4, k2tog) 3 times (15 sts).
Knit 1 round.

Round 165: (K3, k2tog) 3 times (12 sts).
Knit 1 round.

Round 167: (K2, k2tog) 3 times (9 sts).
Cut yarn, leaving a tail, and thread through rem sts.

Spines

Using 3mm needles, and starting at top of head, approximately 2½in (6cm) from mouth end, pick up and knit 92 sts along back, picking up the loop of yarn between each pair of stitches along the centre line; turn and proceed as follows:

*Cast on 2 sts, cast off 3 sts, k2tog, pass first stitch over second stitch on RH needle, transfer st from RH needle to LH needle, rep from * until 11 sts rem, then cast on 3 sts, cast off 5 sts, (transfer st to LH needle, cast on 4 sts, cast off 6 sts) 4 times, fasten off.

Dewlap

Beginning a few rows from end of head and using 3mm needles, pick up and knit 23 sts along underside of head, picking up the loop of yarn between each pair of stitches along the centre line; turn and proceed as follows:

Row 1: *K1, p1, rep from * to last st, k1.

Row 2: K2tog, *p1, k1, rep from * to last st, k1 (22 sts).

Row 3: K1, sl1, k1, psso, *p1, k1, rep from * to last 3 sts, p2tog, k1 (20 sts).

Row 4: Cast off 6 sts in rib, *k1, p1, rep from * to last st, k1 (14 sts).

Row 5: K1, sl1, k1, psso, *k1, p1, rep from * to last 3 sts, k1, k2tog (12 sts).

Row 6: K1, sl1, k1, psso, *p1, k1, rep from * to last 3 sts, p1, k2tog (10 sts).

Row 7: K1, sl1, k1, psso, (k1, p1) twice, k2tog, k1 (8 sts).

Row 8: Cast off 1 st, (k1, p1) 3 times (7 sts).

Row 9: K2tog, k1, p1, k2tog, k1.
Cast off rem 5 sts.

Legs (make 4)

Using 3mm needles and A, cast on 4 sts.
Row 1: Purl.
Row 2: Inc1, k2, inc1 (6 sts).
Row 3: Purl.
Row 4: Cast on 4 sts, k to end (10 sts).
Row 5: Cast on 4 sts, p to end (14 sts).
Beg with a k row, work 18 rows in st st.
Shape knee
Row 24: K12, turn.
Row 25: P10, turn.
Row 26: K9, turn.
Row 27: P8, turn.
Row 28: K7, turn.
Row 29: P6, turn.
Row 30: K5, turn.
Row 31: P4, turn.
Row 32: K3, turn.
Row 33: P to end.
Beg with a k row, work 22 rows in st st.
Cast off.

Back feet

Select two of the legs.
On one of the pieces, with RS facing and cast-on edge uppermost, using 3mm needles, pick up and knit 4 sts (on fourth row), 1 st up side (from end of row 2), 4 sts along cast-on row, 1 st down other side and then the other 4 cast-on sts (14 sts).
Row 2: Purl.
Row 3: K3, k2tog, k4, k2tog, k3 (12 sts).
Row 4: Purl.
Row 5: K5, turn.
Row 6: Purl to end.
Row 7: K4, turn.
Row 8: Purl to end.
Row 9: K3, turn.

Row 10: Purl to end.
Row 11: K2, turn.
Row 12: P5, turn.
Row 13: Knit to end.
Row 14: P4, turn.
Row 15: Knit to end.
Row 16: P3, turn.
Row 17: Knit to end.
Row 18: P2, turn.
Row 19: Knit to end.
Row 20: Purl.
Row 21: Knit.
Row 22: Purl.
Cast off. Complete second back leg in the same way.

Face shield (make 2)

Using 3mm needles and A, cast on 1 st.
Row 1: Inc2 (knit into front, back and front of st) (3 sts).
Row 2: Inc1 in each st (6 sts).
Row 3: Inc1 in each st (12 sts).
Row 4: (K1, inc1) 6 times (18 sts).
Row 5: (K2, inc1) 6 times (24 sts).
Cast off, knitting each st tbl.

Eye piece (make 2)

Using 3mm needles and A, cast on 1 st.
Row 1: Inc2 (knit into front, back and front of st) (3 sts).
Row 2: Inc1 in each st (6 sts).
Row 3: (K1, inc1) 3 times (9 sts).
Row 4: (K1, k2tog) 3 times (6 sts).
Row 5: (K2tog) 3 times (3 sts).
Row 6: Sl1, k2tog, psso; fasten off.

Claws (make 8)

Using 3mm needles and A, cast on 2 sts.
Row 1: K2; do not turn but slide sts to other end of needle.
Rep row 1 23 times more; fasten off.

Making up
Eyes

Stitch eye pieces to sides of head. Insert safety eyes, one through the centre of each of the eye pieces.

Stuffing

Finish stuffing body and head, then pull up tail of yarn at head end and fasten off, closing gap.

Legs

Stitch leg seams using mattress stitch and add stuffing, then pull up yarn to gather seam slightly and cause each leg to bend at knee joint. Sew cast-off edges to body.

Claws

Fold each claw in half and stitch two folded claws to the end of each foot, tucking each fold just inside cast-on edge and using yarn tail to shape foot. Take a few stitches through all layers to flatten each foot slightly.

Head and mouth

Stitch shields to sides of head. With black yarn, embroider a line of backstitch to form mouth.

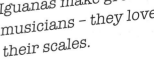

Iguanas make great musicians – they love their scales.

Most snakes range from 3ft (less than 1m) to 33ft (10m) in length. They need a large vivarium – a warm, ventilated, escape-proof home. Snakes eat dinner only once a week: dead mice or rats bought from the pet shop are commonly on the menu.

SNAKE

Information you'll need

Finished size
Snake is approximately 27½in (70cm) long.

Materials
Manos del Uruguay 100% extra-fine
merino kettle-dyed yarn
(219yds/200m per 100g skein)
1 x 100g skein in shade 9644
Chrysanthemum (A)
Small amounts of DK wool yarn in red (B)
and black (C)
Set of four 4mm (UK8:US6) double-
pointed needles
1 pair of 3.25mm (UK10:US3) needles
1 pair of 3.25mm (UK10:US3) double-
pointed needles
Stitch holder
Tapestry needle
Polyester toy filling
Pair of sew-on googly eyes

Tension
This is not critical: just aim for a firm fabric.

DID YOU KNOW?
The smallest snake is the
thread snake – it's the size
of a toothpick!

How to make Snake

Body (in one piece)

Using a set of four 4mm double-pointed needles and A, cast on 6 sts and distribute between three needles; use fourth needle to knit.

Knit 16 rounds.

Round 17: (Inc1, k1) 3 times (9 sts).

Knit 20 rounds.

Add stuffing (and continue to add more stuffing as work progresses).

Round 38: (Inc1, k2) 3 times (12 sts).

Knit 20 rounds.

Round 59: (Inc1, k3) 3 times (15 sts).

Knit 140 rounds.

Shape head

Round 1: (K4, inc1) 3 times (18 sts).

Knit 2 rounds.

Round 4: (K5, inc1) 3 times (21 sts).

Round 5: Knit.

Round 6: (K6, inc1) 3 times (24 sts).

Knit 6 rounds.

Shape mouth

Row 1: K12, turn and transfer rem sts to a stitch holder.

Row 2: Purl.

Row 3: Knit.

Row 4: Purl.

*Row 5: K2, sl1, k1, psso, k4, k2tog, k2 (10 sts).

Beg with a p row, work 3 rows in st st.

Row 9: K2, sl1, k1, psso, k2, k2tog, k2 (8 sts).

Row 10: Purl.

Row 11: K2, sl1, k1, psso, k2tog, k2 (6 sts).

Row 12: Purl.

Cast off.*

Rejoin yarn to sts on holder.

Row 1: Knit.

Row 2: Purl.

Rep from * to *.

DID YOU KNOW?
A snake uses its tongue to smell.

Mouth

Using 3.25mm needles and yarn B, cast on 6 sts.

Row 1: Knit each st tbl.

Row 2: Purl.

Row 3: K1, inc1, k2, inc1, k1 (8 sts).

Row 4: Purl.

Row 5: K1, inc1, k4, inc1, k1 (10 sts).

Beg with a p row, work 9 rows in st st.

Row 15: K2, sl1, k1, psso, k2, k2tog, k2 (8 sts).

Row 16: Purl.

Row 17: K2, sl1, k1, psso, k2tog, k2 (6 sts).

Row 18: Purl.

Cast off.

Tongue

Using two 3.25mm double-pointed needles and C, cast on 2 sts.

Row 1: K2; do not turn but slide sts to other end of needle.

Rep row 1 19 times; cast off.

Fold the piece in half and pick up and knit 2 sts along the fold, then rep row 1 ten times more; cast off.

Making up

You will have been adding stuffing to the main part of the snake; add some more stuffing if necessary, then stitch the mouth to the end of the head, just inside the edge of the main part of the snake. Stitch the tongue firmly to the back of the mouth. Stitch eyes securely in place. (Note: if you prefer, use safety eyes and fix in place before stitching mouth.)

snake

*My snake's good at building
– she's a boa constructor.*

Do goldfish wear fish-knit tights?

Could running hamsters power the lights?

Rabbiting on … do rabbits really talk too much?

Do parrots like carrots?

Techniques

Getting started

Yarns

Most of the pets in this book have been made using double-knitting (US: light worsted) yarn, though other yarns have been introduced where necessary to produce certain details – such as the Tortoise's shell and the Mouse's ear linings. As a general rule, I prefer to use natural fibres in my knitting projects, particularly wool, since it has a natural softness and elasticity. To make these pets really soft and cuddly, either pure wool or wool blends that include other fibres such as cashmere, alpaca and silk have been used throughout the book.

The pattern notes for each pet give the actual yarns used, and in these days of online shopping, it should be easier than ever to source these yarns. If, however, a certain yarn is not available or you decide to substitute your own choice, in order for your pet to be the correct size and shape, it is important that you knit a tension sample before proceeding with the pattern.

Tension (gauge)

To knit a tension sample, cast on 40 stitches using the needle size stated in the pattern and work in stocking stitch (or the stitch stated in the pattern instructions) until your work measures about 5–5½in (12–14cm); cast off loosely. Lay out the piece of knitting on a flat surface and use a ruler (rather than a tape measure) to count the number of stitches and rows over 4in (10cm). If you have more stitches and rows than the number stated in the pattern, you will need to try again, using larger needles; if you have fewer stitches and rows, use smaller needles.

Needles

The needle sizes that have been used throughout the book may seem smaller than you might expect, and will in most cases be smaller than the needles recommended on the yarn's ball band. In general, 3.25mm needles have been used with DK yarn: this is because you are aiming to produce a firm, close-knit fabric that will hold its shape and not allow any stuffing to poke through.

Some of the pets have been knitted using two needles, but most will require you to use four double-pointed needles to knit the component pieces in the round. Two double-pointed needles are used to knit i-cords for various elements such as the Budgie's claws and the Snake's tongue.

Other equipment

A row counter is useful for keeping track of how many rows you have knitted, and rubber point protectors can be slipped on to your needle ends to prevent stitches from slipping off when you put your work down. To hold spare stitches, you will need a stitch holder – though an ordinary safety pin will usually suffice.

A blunt tapestry needle is essential for sewing together pieces of knitting and weaving in yarn ends. A small pair of scissors will be necessary for cutting yarn. You may also find it necessary to use a needle gauge to measure double-pointed needles.

Pattern instructions

Before you start work on your chosen project, it is important to read through the whole pattern, and to make sure you have all the materials and equipment that you will need.

Safety warning

If you are knitting these pets for small children, it is vital that you use safe, clean, new materials. Use your own common sense to guide you. The pets pictured in this book have been stuffed using polyester toy stuffing and safety eyes have been used in most cases. You may prefer to embroider the eyes using spare yarn, in which case, try not to create long loops of yarn that may trap tiny fingers. The Tarantula and Parrot include pipe cleaners, making them unsuitable for small children. Some pets, such as the Kittens and the Guinea pig, have whiskers made from nylon thread, which is also unsuitable for small children, so should be omitted.

Knitting techniques

All the diagrams are shown for right-handed knitters; if you are a left-handed knitter, try holding the diagram in front of a mirror to view it in reverse.

Simple cast–on

This is the main method used throughout the book; some knitters know it as 'two needle' or 'chain' cast-on.

1 Make a slip knot and place it on the left-hand needle. *Insert the right-hand needle into the back of the loop, behind the left-hand needle, and wrap the yarn around it, as shown in the diagram.

2 Use the right-hand needle to pull the yarn through the first loop, creating a new stitch.

3 Transfer this stitch to the left-hand needle and repeat from * until you have the required number of stitches.

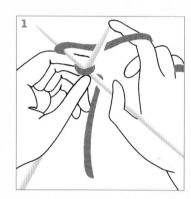

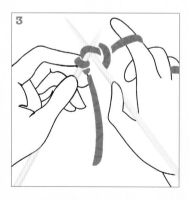

Cable cast-on

This creates a firm edge and can be used as the initial cast-on method or when casting on extra stitches further on in a pattern.

1 Make a slip knot and place it on the left-hand needle. Make one stitch using the simple cast-on method. *For the next stitch, insert the needle between the two stitches on the left-hand needle.

2 Wrap the yarn round the right-hand needle tip and pull through, between the previous two stitches.

3 Transfer the stitch you have made to the left-hand needle and repeat from * until you have the required number of stitches.

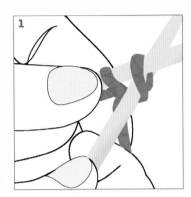

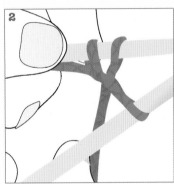

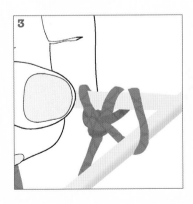

techniques

Knit stitch

Rows of knit stitches produce a garter-stitch fabric; alternating rows of knit and purl stitches produce a stocking stitch fabric – but when knitting in the round, for stocking stitch you use only knit stitches.

These diagrams show work in progress.

1 To make a knit stitch, hold the needle with the stitches in your left hand; insert the tip of the right-hand needle into the first loop, and behind the left-hand needle, and wrap the yarn around it, as shown in the diagram.

2 Use the right-hand needle to pull the yarn towards you, through the first loop, creating a new stitch.

3 Keep this new stitch on the right-hand needle and continue along the row.

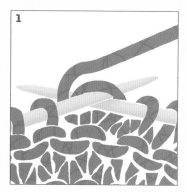

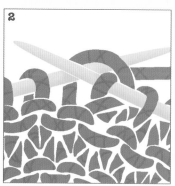

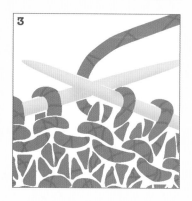

Purl stitch

These diagrams show work in progress.

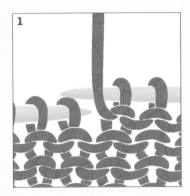

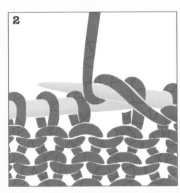

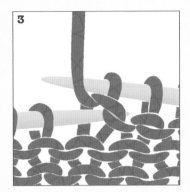

1 To make a purl stitch, begin with the yarn at the front of the work.

2 Insert the tip of the right-hand needle into the front of the next loop, in front of the left-hand needle, and wrap the yarn around it in an anti-clockwise direction.

3 Use the right-hand needle to pull the yarn through the first loop, creating a new stitch. Keep this new stitch on the right-hand needle and continue along the row.

Knitted fabrics

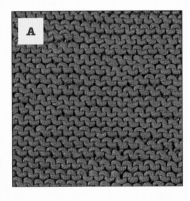

Garter stitch (A)
Knit every row.

Stocking stitch (B)
Alternate between knit and purl rows.

Casting off

This is usually done using knit stitches, although occasionally you will be required to cast off in purl. To avoid confusion, and make it clear which method to use, the pattern instructions will tell you to cast off 'knitwise' or 'purlwise'.

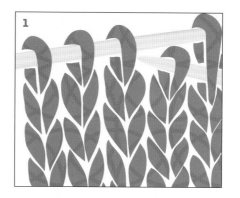

1 Knit the first two stitches on to the right-hand needle. Then, using the tip of the left-hand needle, slip the first stitch over the second stitch, leaving just one stitch on the right-hand needle.

2 Knit another stitch so that there are two stitches on the right-hand needle, and repeat the process until there is only one stitch left. Cut the yarn and thread the end of the yarn through the remaining stitch to fasten off.

Shaping

Increases

Increases are worked in one of three ways:

- by casting on extra stitches at the beginning of a row

- by knitting into an existing stitch twice or three times – referred to in the pattern as inc1 or inc2

- by making an extra stitch by picking up the horizontal loop of yarn between the needles, placing it on the left-hand needle and knitting (or purling, where stated) into the back of the stitch – referred to in the pattern as M1.

Knitting note

Where the pattern states 'inc1', knit into the front and back of the stitch, thereby creating one extra stitch. Where the pattern states 'inc2', knit into the front, the back and the front again, creating two extra stitches.

Decreases

Decreases are worked in a number of different ways:

- **k2tog** Insert the right-hand needle into the front loops of the next two stitches and knit both stitches together.

- **k2tog tbl** Insert the right-hand needle into the back loops of the next two stitches and knit both stitches together.

- **sl1, k1, psso** Slip the next stitch on to the right-hand needle, knit the next stitch, then using the tip of the left-hand needle, slip the slipped stitch over the knitted stitch.

- **p2tog** With the yarn at the front of the work, insert the right-hand needle into the front loops of the next two stitches and purl both stitches together.

- **p3tog** With the yarn at the front of the work, insert the right-hand needle into the front loops of the next three stitches and purl all three stitches together.

Gathering

Another way of creating shape is by gathering, usually at the making-up stage. To gather stitches – for example, when you are shaping a neck between body and head – stitch a running stitch through the stitches of a single row, using matching yarn, then pull up to the required width.

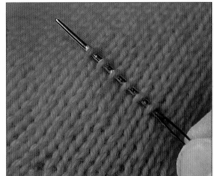

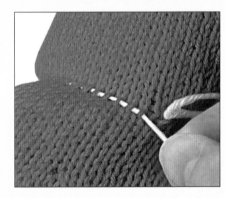

Knitting in the round

Some of the knitted components needed to make up each pet are knitted flat, using two needles, and stitched together to create three-dimensional shapes, while many of the components are knitted 'in the round' on four needles. Knitting on four needles can be tricky, especially when you are working the first few rows. To cast on, use the two-needle 'simple' method, since it will create a firm, tight edge that is less likely to slip off the needles. For some of the pattern pieces, you will see that the first row or round is knitted by inserting the needle into the back loop of each stitch, which also helps to form a firm edge.

Picking up stitches

Sometimes the instructions require you to 'pick up and knit' stitches – for example, along the back of the Iguana. Use the needle to pick up a loop of yarn between stitches, wrap the yarn around it and use the right-hand needle to pull the yarn towards you, through the loop, to create a new stitch, just as you do when knitting a row of stitches. Pick up the next loop of yarn to the left and repeat the process until you have picked up the required number of stitches.

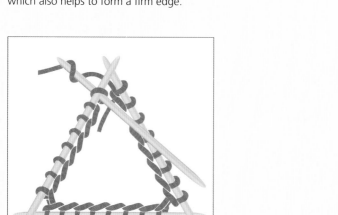

Making an i-cord

The i-cord is a knitted cord that can be made up of two or more stitches. In this book, i-cords are used in various ways – to make a tongue for the Snake or toes for the Iguana, for example.

Using two double-pointed needles, cast on the number of stitches stated in the pattern and knit these stitches. Do not turn the work but slide the stitches to the opposite end of the right-hand needle, transfer this needle to the other hand and, taking the yarn firmly across the back of the work, knit the stitches. Repeat the process until the cord is the desired length.

Making up

When working on a small scale, the objective is to be as neat as possible, as untidy or clumsy sewing will spoil the appearance of your pet. When joining the sides of two knitted pieces – the row ends – it is advisable to use one of two methods: mattress stitch or backstitch. When joining two straight edges – a cast-on edge to a cast-off edge – oversew the edges for a neat result.

Mattress-stitch seam

This method creates an invisible seam.

1 Thread a blunt needle with a long length of matching yarn. With the right sides of the work facing, place the two edges together.

2 Starting at the bottom edge of the work, insert the needle under the bar between the first and second stitches on the right-hand side.

3 Insert the needle in the same way on the opposite edge.

4 Repeat, working across from left to right and back again, moving up the seam. Do not pull stitches tight.

5 When you reach the top of the seam, pull the yarn ends until the two sides meet. Do not pull too tightly or you will cause the seam to pucker. Fasten off the yarn ends securely.

Backstitch seam

1 Thread a blunt needle with a long length of matching yarn. Place the two pieces to be joined on top of one another, right sides together.

2 Working from right to left, one stitch in from selvedge, bring the needle up through both layers then back down through both layers one row to the left.

3 Bring the needle back up through both layers one row to the left, then back down one row to the right, in the same place as before.

4 Repeat, taking the needle two rows to the left each time, and one row back.

Backstitch is sometimes used for sewing facial features too, for example, the Iguana's mouth.

Oversewing

Line up the edges to be joined and whipstitch together on the right side of the work.

Finishing touches

There is a bit more to making a knitted pet than simply knitting the component parts and stitching them together. You can subtly alter the angle of a head or the positioning of legs, ears or wings, for example. Then there is the way you embroider features such as noses or tufts of hair. Take care when stuffing your pet, using plenty of stuffing to create a firm result but not overstuffing so much that you distort the shape or cause excess stuffing to poke through the knitted fabric.

Embroidery

Thread a blunt needle with a single strand of yarn in the colour required. Insert the needle into an inconspicuous point, such as the nape of the neck, and bring it through the work to the point where you wish to add embroidery stitches, so that the end of the yarn is lost inside the stuffing.

Bullion stitch
A decorative embroidery stitch made by winding the thread several times around the needle before sewing a backstitch. Used for details such as the Hamster's tail.

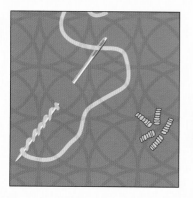

Fly stitch
Bring the needle up through the fabric at the top left, then insert the needle back through the fabric to the right, then back up through the fabric halfway between the first two points but slightly lower down, ensuring that the tip of the needle emerges under the loop of thread. Pull up, to form a u-shape, then take needle back through the fabric a little lower down, to form a straight stitch that holds the loop of thread in place. Useful for features such as the hamster's mouth.

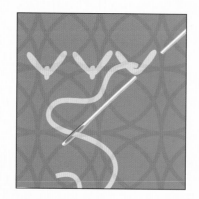

Satin stitch
Use this filling-in stitch for noses. Bring the needle to one edge of the area you wish to embroider then work straight stitches, close together, to fill in the area.

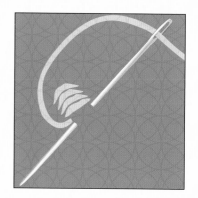

Straight stitch
As the name implies, this is a single straight stitch. In this book, it is used to create simple details such as a mouth or whisker.

Chain stitch

This stitch is used to decorate the Tortoise's shell. Bring the needle up at the point you wish your row of chain stitches to begin; then reinsert it down through the same point, creating a loop of yarn. Bring the needle back out through the knitted fabric a little way along and inside the loop. Pull the yarn, not too tightly, to create the first chain stitch, then reinsert the needle at the place where it last emerged and repeat to form a row of linked chain stitches.

Swiss darning

This is a type of embroidery that replicates the knitted stitch; it is sometimes easier than incorporating motifs into the work as you knit. It has been used to create patches on the body and legs of the Puppy.

If you look at a row of knitting, you will see that each stitch resembles a 'V'. Thread a blunt needle with yarn and bring it up through the point of the V, then take it behind the two prongs of the V and back down into the point where you began. This stitch is useful for embroidering a small mouth.

Hair

To create a tuft of hair – such as the one on top of the Guinea pig's head – make a bundle of yarn by wrapping yarn around two or more fingers, then tying firmly around the centre. Stitch the centre of the bundle to the head very securely. For a soft, wispy effect, separate the strands of thread by running a blunt needle from the base of each strand to the tip. Trim yarn ends to the desired length.

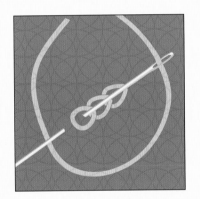

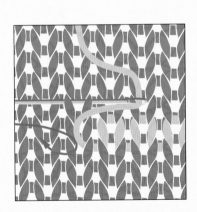

Abbreviations

alt	alternate
cm	centimetre(s)
in	inch(es)
inc1	knit into front and back of next stitch
inc2	knit into front, back and front of same stitch
k	knit
k2tog	knit two stitches together
m1	pick up the loop between the last and the next stitch and knit into the back of it
psso	pass slipped stitch over
p	purl
p2tog	purl two stitches together
rem	remain(ing)
rep	repeat
RS	right side
sl1	slip one stitch
st (s)	stitch(es)
st st	stocking stitch
tbl	through back of loop
tog	together
WS	wrong side
( )	repeat instructions inside brackets as many times as instructed

Conversions
Knitting needles

UK:	Metric:	US:
14	2mm	0
13	2.25mm	1
12	2.75mm	2
11	3mm	–
10	3.25mm	3
–	3.5mm	4
9	3.75mm	5
8	4mm	6
7	4.5mm	7
6	5mm	8
5	5.5mm	9
4	6mm	10
3	6.5mm	10.5
2	7mm	10.5
1	7.5mm	11
0	8mm	11
00	9mm	13
000	10mm	15

UK/US yarn weights

UK:	US:
2-ply	Lace
3-ply	Fingering
4-ply	Sport
Double knitting (DK)	Light worsted
Aran	Fisherman/ worsted
Chunky	Bulky
Super chunky	Extra bulky

Yarn suppliers

Artesano Ltd
Unit G, Lamb's Farm Business Park
Basingstoke Road
Swallowfield
Reading
Berkshire
RG7 1PQ
Tel: +44 (0)118 9503350
www.artesanoyarns.co.uk

Coats Crafts UK
Green Lane Mill
Holmfirth
West Yorkshire
HD9 2DX
Tel: +44 (0)1484 681881
www.coatscrafts.co.uk

Cygnet Yarns Ltd
12–14 Adelaide Street
Bradford
West Yorkshire
BD5 0EF
Tel: +44 (0)1274 743374
www.cygnetyarns.com

Debbie Bliss
Designer Yarns Ltd
Unit 8–10
Newbridge Industrial Estate
Pitt Street
Keighley
West Yorkshire
BD21 4PQ
Tel: +44 (0)1535 664222
www.designeryarns.uk.com

King Cole Ltd
Merrie Mills
Elliott Street
Silsden
West Yorkshire
BD20 0DE
Tel: +44 (0)1535 650230
www.kingcole.co.uk

MillaMia UK
Studio 11
32 Bolton Gardens
London
SW5 0AQ
Tel: +44 8450 177474
www.millamia.com

Rowan Yarns Ltd
Green Lane Mill
Holmfirth
West Yorkshire
HD9 2DX
Tel: +44 (0)1484 681881
www.knitrowan.com

About the author

Having studied Fine Art at the Slade School, Susie Johns began her publishing career as a magazine and partworks editor before becoming a freelance writer and designer. She is the author of more than 30 craft books on a range of subjects including knitting, crochet, papier mâché and embroidery. Susie has also contributed to a number of magazines, such as *Let's Knit*, *Crafts Beautiful*, *Embroidery*, *Needlecraft*, *Woman's Weekly*, *Family Circle*, *Practical Parenting* and *Art Attack* and has made several television appearances demonstrating various crafts. She particularly enjoys art and craft activities that involve recycling and reinventing. Susie is a qualified teacher and runs workshops in drawing and painting, knitting and crochet, embroidery, and 3D design. She is the founder member of the East Greenwich knitting group, 'Knitting Night at The Pelton'.

Author acknowledgements

Thanks to Coats Patons, King Cole, Rowan, Artesano, Cygnet and Designer Yarns (Debbie Bliss) for supplying the yarns used throughout this book.

A big 'thank you' to Gerrie Purcell at GMC for asking me to do the book in the first place, to Virginia Brehaut for managing the project so patiently, to Helen Tomes and Cath Senker for meticulous pattern checking, Rob Janes for designing such eye-catching pages and Anthony Bailey for the photography.

Finally, a long-lasting 'thank you' to my children for their invaluable patience, support and feedback.